TUNING
TO
WIN

TUNING
TO
WIN

Ian Pinnell

with Tim Davison

FERNHURST
BOOKS

62 Brandon Parade, Holly Walk, Leamington Spa, Warwickshire, CV32 4JE, UK
Tel: +44 (0) 1926 337488 | www.fernhurstbooks.com

A catalogue record for this book is available from the British Library
ISBN 978-1-909911-48-2

All photographs © Fernhurst Books Limited or Pinnell & Bax, except:
p15 (right) © Selden; p19 (right) © Mark Dunkley; p53, 62, 67 © Lee Whitehead; p60, 64, 66, 68, 73 © Tim Olin; p76, 77 (left) © Alistair Mackay; p79 © Tom Gruitt

Front cover photograph © Christophe Favreau

Designed by Rachel Atkins
Illustrated by Maggie Nelson
Printed in China through World Print

IAN PINNELL

MULTIPLE CHAMPION, SAILMAKER & CHANDLER

Ian Pinnell first learnt to sail at Dorman Long Sailing Club on Teeside aged 10 in 1971. He progressed to Tees Sailing Club, began winning races and became a sailmaker at Storrar & Bax. This business started off in Newcastle and then moved to Northampton and was renamed Pinnell & Bax.

The business has moved from initially being a sailmaker to now having five departments: manufacturing & sailmaking, shop & mail order, repair, rigging and new boats.

Ian has been winning championships since the early 1980s and is continuing to do so over 30 years later. He has over 40 World, European or National Championship titles to his name in classes as diverse as the Enterprise, 505 and Mumm 30.

World Championships
505
Enterprise (x 4)
Fireball (x 2)

European Championships
505 (x 3)
Fireball (x 5)

National Championships
505 (x 11)
Enterprise (x 2)
Fireball (x 8)
Miracle (x 2)
Mumm 30 (Tactician) (x 2)
National 12 (x 2)

Ian was co-author of *Helming to Win* with Lawrie Smith in the original *Sail to Win* series. He is the only sailor to have written a book in both the original and new series, confirming his longevity at the top of dinghy sailing.

CONTENTS

FOREWORD

Whether you race an Optimist, Laser, Finn, Star or America's Cup foiling catamaran (or anything in between) there are two things that will determine your results: the skill of the sailors and the way your boat is set up. The former is determined by latent talent and training, the latter is more complex. Tuning a boat to give you maximum boatspeed is not easy. There are so many variables to consider – it is multidimensional.

In my sailing career I have been lucky enough to work with the best. Pre-eminent among them is, of course, Andrew 'Bart' Simpson. As Bob Fisher stated in his obituary in The Guardian:

"All sailors have their specialities: Simpson's extended from his search for speed into the nuts and bolts of how it might be obtained. His meticulous boat preparation was second to none... Simpson spent many hours working on their Star and was rewarded with unsurpassed boat performance".

It is only fitting that this new book in the *Sail to Win* series, about boat tuning, is supporting the Andrew Simpson Sailing Foundation.

Ian Pinnell, who has won more championships than most of us can dream of, explains with clear text, photographs and diagrams how to tune your dinghy for maximum boatspeed. Once you have that, you can concentrate on your own performance.

Good luck!

Iain Percy
2 x Olympic gold medallist, 1 x Olympic silver medallist, 3 x World Champion, 3 x America's Cup challenger

INTRODUCTION

Boatspeed is a vital ingredient in winning, but many races are won by only a few boat lengths or seconds. Given that most dinghy races last somewhere between 30 minutes and an hour, you are talking about tiny difference in boatspeed. A 30-second lead in a 30-minute race only equates to the winner going less than 2% faster than the other boat!

We are talking about fine margins here and small changes to your boat's tuning can easily make that sort of difference to your boatspeed.

This book will help you understand how the rig and foils generate boatspeed. It will show you how to alter the controls to power up or down, depending on wind strength, and how to alter the rig for upwind and downwind sailing. In short, it aims to give you blinding speed and get you pointing so high that you never need to sail on port tack!

The book is organised into three parts:

Part 1: Getting Ready
Focussing on what needs to be done or known before you start tuning, this section begins with how to assemble a hull, foils and gear so that you have compatible kit to tune. Every bit of standard rigging (the things you set up ashore) is then explained, moving onto the effects of the control lines (the ropes you tweak as you sail round the course).

Not every type of boat will have all the equipment and controls described here, but that doesn't matter, you can just learn how to use the ones that you do have!

Part 2: Tuning
The second part of the book covers boat tuning itself, beginning with the initial set up (which is always for light wind beating), and going on to modifying this set up for beating in medium and strong winds, along with information on reaching and running.

A section on two boat tuning details how you can refine your settings even further, and a dedicated troubleshooting section will help pull you back from the brink when it's all gone horribly wrong.

Part 3: Skills
The last section of the book covers all the skills you need to make the boat work, be it splicing control lines, replacing a slot gasket or threading a new halyard through the mast.

Armed with this knowledge you will have the confidence to get in the groove right from the start, be able to concentrate on all the other things that need your attention in a race, and work your way up the leaderboard!

GETTING READY

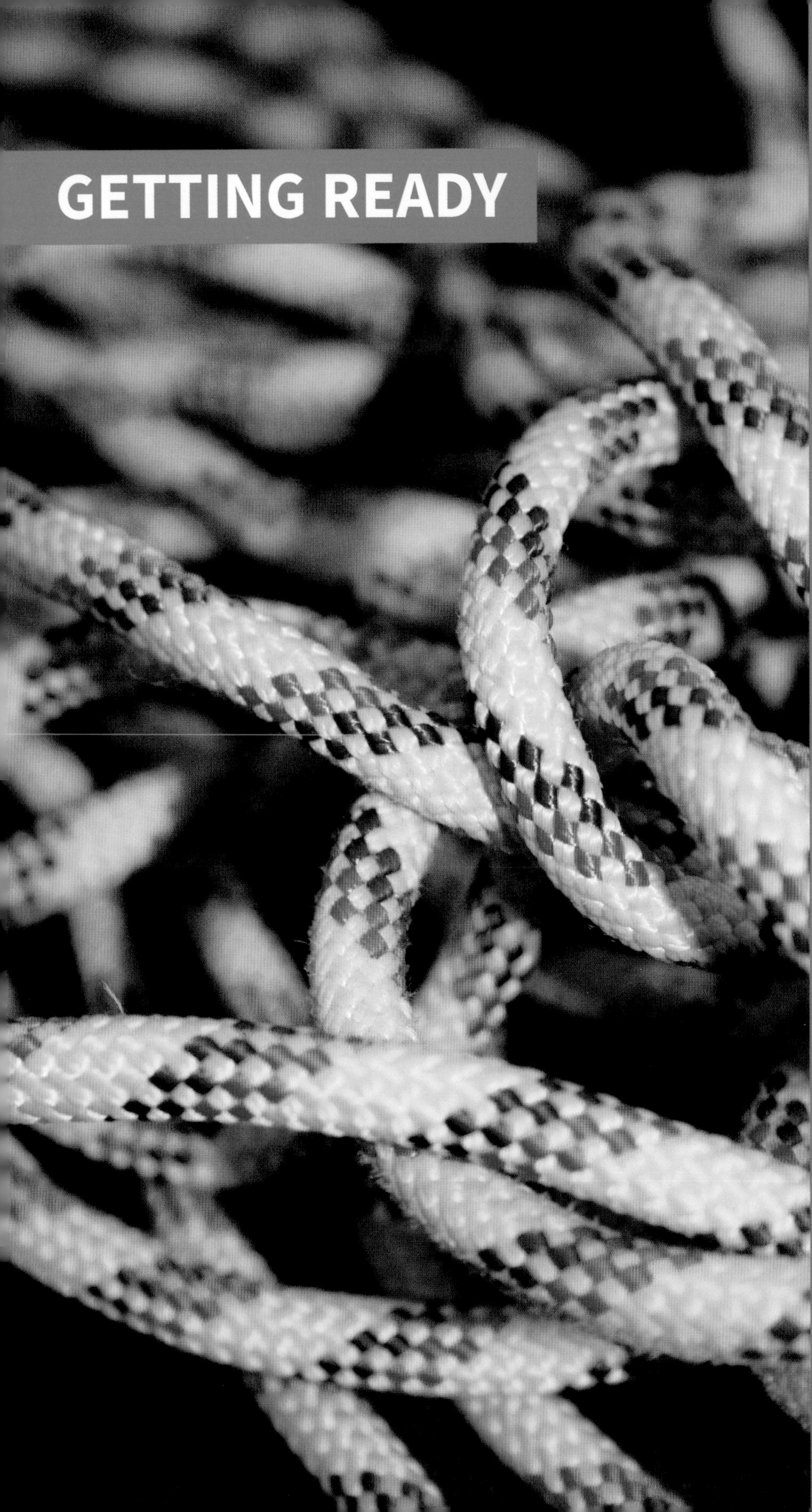

PART 1

Assembling The Gear

Your first decision is whether to buy new or second-hand. Provided you buy from an expert builder, a new boat should have systems that work, are calibrated and are less likely to fail. The sails are new and the boat should be fast right out of the box. If not, the builder will give you advice and support. Of course, this all comes at a cost – it is very time consuming to fit out a new boat. (For example, it takes our team at P&B 55 hours to set up a 505, and an amateur would probably take twice as long.)

A second-hand boat will be cheaper, and may be fast if you buy a proven boat or can re-tune an unsuccessful one. If you aren't in a hurry then a cheap boat will give you an introduction to the class and a better idea of what you want when you do move on to a new boat.

Buying A New Boat

Unless the manufacturer supplies a complete boat, you will need to buy the hull, foils, spars and sails.

The Hull

You must buy the hull from someone who is an expert in the class, particularly if you want them to fit it out. Look for:

- Championship results
- Build quality
- Quality of finish
- Under weight

Foils

The rudder wants to be as small as you can handle, to give less drag. It must be stiff.

The centreboard should be stiff in light / medium winds but have enough flex to depower in a gust. How much it needs to flex depends on your crew weight – the lighter you are the more it should flex. Check this by clamping the board, hanging a 15 kg weight on the tip and comparing it with others (right). The spec of the laminate alters the board's stiffness. If yours turns out to be the wrong stiffness for your weight, you may need a new board.

Think long and hard about the slot gasket, which is vital for speed. It must be in good condition and tensioned properly (which also improves the seal around the board).

Checking centreboard stiffness

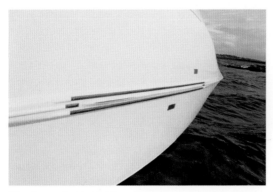

The slot gasket is vital for speed

Mast

The first decision is carbon or aluminium. If the class rules allow, go for carbon every time. These masts have a smaller section, are lighter and recover from big loadings (e.g. hitting the bottom in a capsize) better than their metal counterparts.

Unfortunately, carbon spars cost 2-3 times more and don't like having holes drilled in them.

Next choose your mast manufacturer, if necessary in conjunction with your sailmaker. There may be a number of sections to choose from: go for the one that best suits your crew weight by asking the mast supplier.

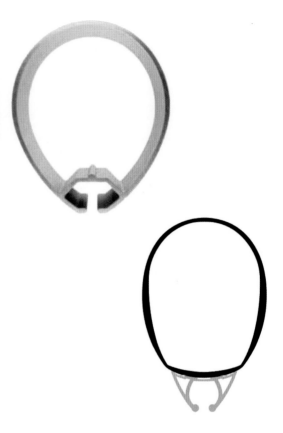

Aluminium (top) and carbon (bottom) cross sections

Section	Illustration	Sailor Weight	Stiffness F/A	Stiffness Athwart	Description
C Sleeved		< 75 kg	14.1	9.8	The mast for the lighter members of the fleet, giving greater flexibility and bend.
D Plus		75-90 kg	20.0	13.8	Perfect all-rounder for the Solo, providing good gust response and flexibility for the rougher sea states with enough stiffness to maximise pointing in the flatter inland venues.
Cumulus		> 90 kg	20.4	14.4	Stiffer than C section up to the hounds, but flexible fore and aft, and stiff sideways in the topmast. For heavier sailors.

The table illustrates various Solo masts available from Selden

Sails

Choose a sailmaker who has good results in your class, has good tuning data and offers a good service.

He will cut the sail to fit your mast, crew weight and the expected conditions.

Heavier cloth lasts longer but, of course, gives weight aloft. Lighter cloth gives more speed initially, but wears out quicker. And remember, Dacron stretches with use whereas Mylar shrinks, so don't mix them!

Crosscut sails are simple to make. Radial sails are more complex, but each panel has the warp lined up with the direction of stress so the sails are more stable. As a result they can be made in lighter cloth, but they are more expensive.

If you're unhappy with a sail, your sailmaker can re-cut the luff. One or two centimetres here makes a big difference, and he will seldom need to adjust the panels.

Since the key variations are so small, I'm afraid you won't learn much by laying the sail out yourself on a flat surface. Leave the analysis to your friendly sailmaker.

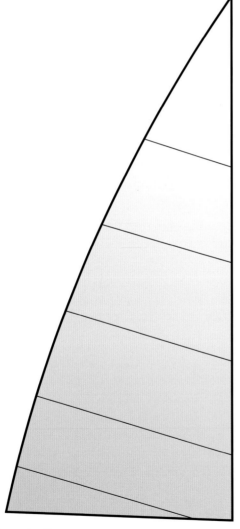

Crosscut sail

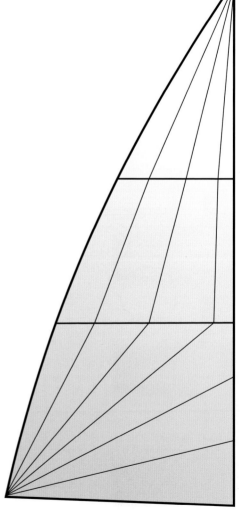

Radial sail

Buying A Second-Hand Boat

If you can afford it, buy a proven boat. You'll know it's fast, and the seller will give you the settings. If you get on well he might even help you at regattas.

If you can't find a boat with a winning record, you will have to look at whatever is on the market. Go back to the manufacturer for the boat's history, then check the boat's condition yourself. Pay particular attention to:

- The finish of the hull and foils, and the fit of the slot gasket.
- The weight of the hull: check this yourself to the best of your ability. Be suspicious if there are no correctors, indeed you should really only buy a boat *with* correctors.
- The rig set-up (see Part 2). For example, check that the spreaders are symmetrical and that the mast isn't bent sideways but does bend evenly fore and aft.
- The sails.

Spread the main and jib on the floor and look for signs of the cloth breaking down. Creases are suspicious, as is marbling (white crazing lines,

below). Examine the clew area of the jib and area around the inboard ends of the main's batten pockets.

Hold the spinnaker out horizontally by the corners and check the cloth. Do the leeches look tighter than the rest of the sail? The sail will stretch with age but the leeches won't. If you have a sail like this you'll probably need a new one.

Hopefully though, everything will be ok, in which case you're in business!

If the leeches are tighter than the rest of the sail it has stretched and needs replacing

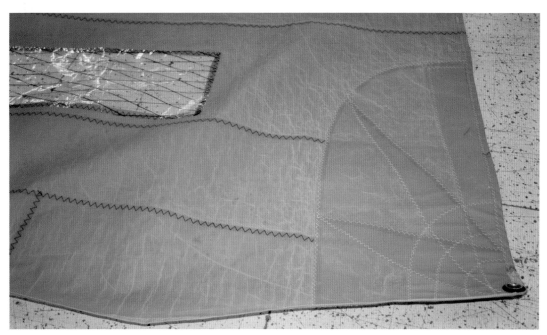

Marbling is an indication of the cloth breaking down and the need for a new sail

What Each Control Does

You are now the proud owner of a boat, no doubt covered in multi-coloured control lines. Surely, you think, I don't need all this string?!

...I'm afraid you do. The ability to tune the rig ashore, and then tweak it afloat, is vital to your success.

This chapter looks at what each control does. I've divided it into two parts:
1. The standing rigging, spreaders, chocks and so on that you tend to set up ashore.
2. The control lines that you are constantly adjusting afloat, e.g. the vang, mainsheet, etc.

Standing Rigging

The Sails

When laid out on its own the sail is flat, with a curved luff

When set on a straight mast there is a belly in the sail

When the mast bends it takes out most of the belly

The sailmaker should have cut the sails to fit your mast and your crew weight. That is to say the luff curve needs to match the mast's bend characteristics, and the fullness in the sail matches the power you need. (Light crews need flatter sails than their heavy rivals.)

Usually you will only have one set of sails, designed to cover the wind range (say from 4 to 22 knots). You will have to tune and tweak the rig to get the sails working in light, medium and strong winds.

However, if you can afford it, or are determined to win (and the class rules allow), you will need a sail wardrobe:

- 2 spinnakers – one small and flat for heavy air, another large and full for light winds.
- 2 mains – one flat, one full.
- 2 jibs – one flat, one full.

Full sails give power

Flatter sails give less drag

Sails for light and medium winds give power and can be set up for pointing. Heavy air sails are cut flatter to give less drag, and give boatspeed via flatness and open leeches.

If you can't afford two sets, at least have stiffer battens for strong winds, which keep the sail flatter and give the wind a better exit from the leech.

Note that some people like to use their old sails in strong winds, but this is doubly wrong: old sails will have become fuller, and the draft will have moved aft – exactly what you don't want. I'm afraid it's a fact of life that sails do wear out, and you won't win with old sails.

If you want to be in the top ten nationally you will probably need one new mainsail, two jibs and two spinnakers per year. If you're going for the Olympics, the sky's the limit. In our Soling Olympic campaign we kept a log of hours use and conditions for each sail, and replaced it when its time was up. To quote one triallist (needless to say a sailmaker): "Six races and they're absolutely shot!" A club sailor should really get new sails every season although, depending on your use, you might be able to stretch to a new set every two to three years.

Preserve your sails by avoiding flogging – e.g. heave-to between races. You can use your second set for club racing, but use the best sails for two boat tuning (see p76).

Even in light airs, try to avoid your sails flogging between races

Telltales

Since you can't see the wind, use telltales (pieces of wool or thin strips of spinnaker sail cloth) to show how the wind is moving over the sails.

Main Telltales

On a boat with a jib, you only need leech telltales on the main. These are usually sown into the batten pockets. When beating, concentrate on the top one. Pull on the vang until it stalls 30-50% of the time in a two-sail boat and 70% in a one-sailed boat:

- If it streams all the time, the leech is too open.
- If it stalls all the time, the leech is too tight.

In smooth water the leech can be tighter than in rough seas. Also faster boats need more twist, slower boats less twist. You guage all of these by the top leech telltale.

   A one-sail boat will have luff telltales too, which would be positioned about 30-35 cm behind the luff, which help you judge when the boat is 'on the wind'.

Jib Telltales

The jib has a leech telltale which helps you judge the wind through the slot. Aim to have it streaming around 70% of the time:

- If it streams all the time, the leech is open. This will give good sailing speed, but may hinder pointing.
- If it stalls all the time, the leech is too closed (too tight) and the airflow is stalling.

The jib will also have three pairs of luff telltales, 20-25 cm back from the luff. Turn into the wind and all three to windward should lift at the same time:

- If the top one breaks first, the leech is too twisted – sheet in or move the lead forward.
- If the bottom one breaks first, the leech is too tight – loosen the sheet or move the lead aft.

Of course, the helmsman also uses these three jib telltales to steer 'on the wind'.

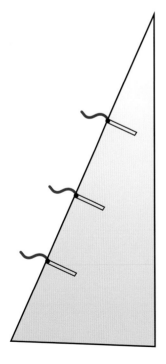

Main telltales on a boat with a jib

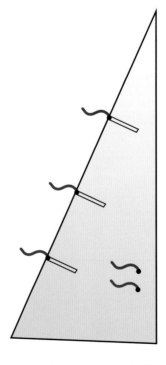

Main telltales on a single-sailed boat

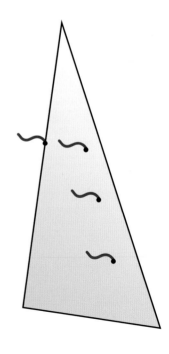

*Luff and leech **telltales** on a jib*

Battens

Battens are there to keep the leech exit flat and to help support the roach. In windy conditions, use stiffer battens to keep the leech straight. In light airs the battens can be softer.

The battens should be under tension to eliminate vertical creases. This is achieved either by elastic at the inboard end of the batten pocket or by a tensioning device at the outboard end.

The lower battens are tapered, with the bendy end forward. A full sail requires more taper.

> ### TOP TIP
>
> **If you get a crease from the clew to the inward end of the bottom batten, this is caused by the excessive roach which the batten can't support. You can either try using a batten with a bendier inboard end, or re-cut the leech.**

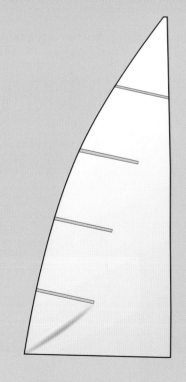

Crease from clew to lower batten

Top batten too slack, resulting in vertical creases through the full length of the batten

Correct tension

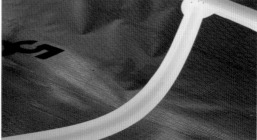

Too much tension on top batten, inducing bend into the batten and making the mainsail too full

Some sails are fully battened. They are cut so that the flow at the top is at 50% aft. At the bottom, the flow is about 33% aft. The batten tapers reflect this.

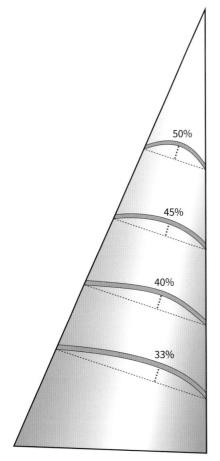

With fully battened sails the position of flow differs with height

Note that the top batten is not tapered because it needs a symmetrical bend (50% aft). It generally has a more sophisticated tensioning device (string, Velcro or a rocket device – which is adjusted with a screwdriver). Note that you **cannot** tune the camber by pushing it in harder or softer – this has minimal effect. Simply push in the batten until the material is just taught.

If you want to adjust the camber, use a stiffer batten to make the top of the sail flatter, or a bendy batten to increase the camber there.

The Mast Step

In most classes the mast step is set at the right place, then everything else is adjusted around it. Your sailmaker will give you the position, usually defined as the distance from the back of the mast to the outside of the transom (through the transom flaps). The position depends on where the centreboard bolt is located in the boat, because you are trying to get the centre of effort of the rig above the centre of lateral resistance of the hull and centreboard (below).

You can, of course, move the whole rig towards the bow by moving the mast foot forward. This reduces weather helm. It can also give good speed in light airs. Conversely, moving the whole rig back increases weather helm. Simply moving the mast foot forward (and not the rest of the rig) increases rake.

Mast step in correct position: Boat in balance

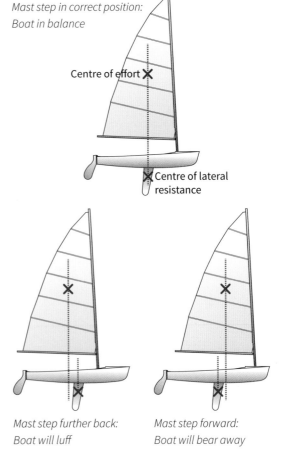

Mast step further back: Boat will luff

Mast step forward: Boat will bear away

The Forestay & Jib Halyard

On a dinghy with a jib, the forestay is simply there to hold up the mast when the sails are down. When the sails are up, the jib halyard is holding the mast forward.

The jib halyard (or forestay if you have no jib) controls the rake of the mast. The shrouds do not control the rake, they control the rig tension.

Increasing the rake:

1. Bends the mast (via the spreaders or mast gate), giving a flatter mainsail with a more open leech.
2. Moves the centre of effort aft, giving more weather helm. (Balance this by raising the centreboard, thus moving the centre of lateral resistance aft.)

The Shrouds

The shrouds set the rig tension.

It's fast in strong winds to crank up the tension, but in some boats (like the 470) excessive tension bends the hull – so be careful not to put on too much. In classes with bendy rigs too much tension may bend the mast too early.

Ideally, the jib halyard and the shrouds should be adjusted together to keep the rig tension constant – i.e. as you let off the jib halyard you want to tighten the shrouds. But in some classes, like the Solo, you are not allowed to alter the shrouds afloat, so if you want to rake the mast back on the water all you can do is take out the fast pin to lengthen the forestay and accept that the rig tension will be lower.

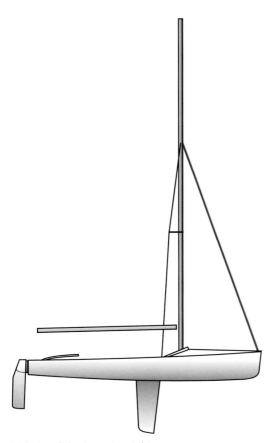

Jib halyard short, mast upright

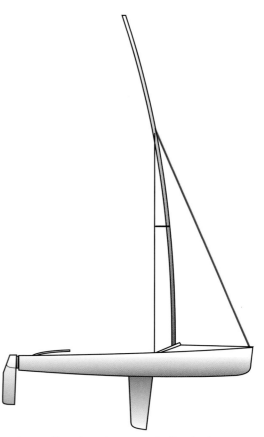

Jib halyard lengthened, mast is raked back. The shrouds are tightened as the jib halyard is lengthened

23

The Spreaders
The spreaders control the mast bend in two directions: sideways and fore and aft.

The spreaders support the middle of the mast and help prevent the mast bending sideways. The longer the spreaders, the more support they give, making the mast stiffer sideways. This works even when the leeward shroud is slack.

The spreaders are angled aft, and the angle helps reduce or increase mast bend fore and aft. The spreaders are usually angled slightly forward of the direct line from the hounds to the shroud base. This gives a stiff mast.

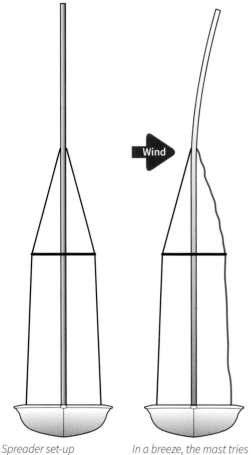

Spreader set-up   *In a breeze, the mast tries to bend to leeward. This is resisted by the windward shroud pushing on the spreader*

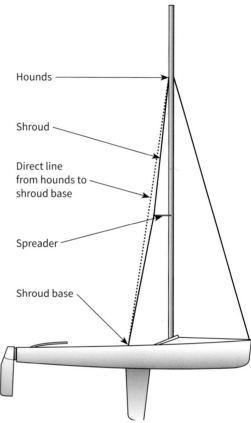

Hounds

Shroud

Direct line from hounds to shroud base

Spreader

Shroud base

Spreaders are angled slightly forward of the dotted line. This stiffens the mast

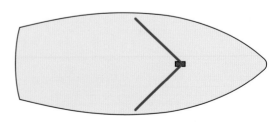

The spreaders are in their initial position

As the spreaders are angled back, the shroud tension pushes the spreaders towards the mast, inducing fore-and-aft bend in the middle of the mast.

Angling the spreaders back moves the mast forward and the resulting bend makes the sail flatter.

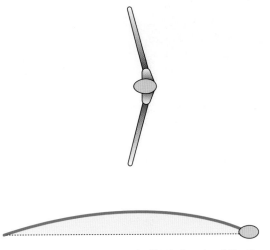

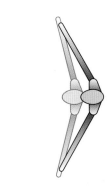

Before the spreaders are angled back there is a full sail

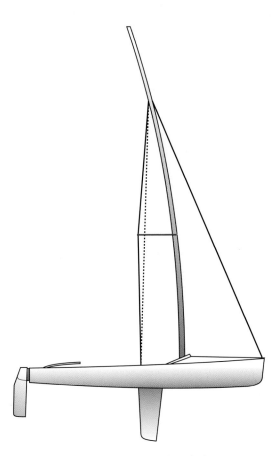

Raking the spreaders further back bends the mast

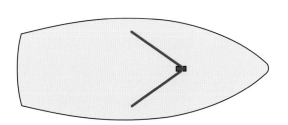

These spreaders are angled further back

As the spreaders move back the mast moves forward, leading to a flatter sail due to more mast bend

Note that if the spreader angle is kept constant, more bend is induced when the mast is raked back. (If you don't want this, angle the spreaders further forward.)

Mast Gate / Strut

The lower mast of your boat may be controlled either by chocks in the mast gate or a strut, which does the same job.

Mast strut

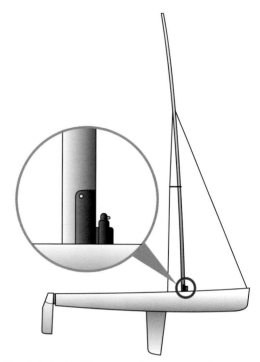

Chocks in front of the mast reduce mast bend

The fore-and-aft bend in the lower third of the mast is controlled by putting chocks into the front of the mast gate or by adjusting the strut. Adding more chocks in front of the mast (or pulling the strut down) straightens the mast; removing chocks (or loosening the strut) allows fore-and-aft bend.

In light airs you may need to pre-bend the mast to flatten the main and open the leech. This is achieved by:
• Sweeping the spreaders back, or
• Reducing the chocks in front of the mast and adding chocks behind it (back chocking).

For example, in the Solo you would have 3 positions with the chocks:
• In light airs you want the mast forward and would use a small (5 mm) chock to encourage mast bend.
• In medium airs you would have a 10 mm chock to straighten the mast.
• In heavy airs you want the mast to bend more. More rake would achieve this and, if so, you would have chocks of 10-15 mm. If the rake isn't increased you will need to decrease the size of the chocks to get more mast bend.

Removing chocks from in front of the mast increases bend in the lower third of the mast

Lowers

Lowers run from the gooseneck area (or above) to the shroud base. **They help control fore-and-aft and sideways bend in the gooseneck area, and resist the bending effect of the vang – particularly on a reach.**

When *beating* control the bend in the lower mast like this:

- In light winds let the lowers right off.
- In medium winds pull them on.
- In strong winds pull them even harder, and tighten them further if you rake the mast aft.

Offwind you generally leave the lowers in the beating position. But if you want to power up on a reach pull them on further.

Single-Handers

The Solo has shrouds but no spreaders. The forestay length controls the rake, and the chocks control mast bend. As you rake further back you need more chocks in front of the mast.

Unstayed boats like the Laser and Topper have no fixed controls. Advice for tuning these boats is almost the opposite of that given above:

- You can only use the vang and cunningham to create mast bend.
- In light winds put on some kicker to bend the mast and flatten the sail's entry. Let out some mainsheet to get the boom out on the quarter.
- In strong winds pull on the vang and cunningham hard, sometimes as hard as you can.

———— Lowers

———— Vang

STERN VIEW

Wind

Leeward lower

On a beat, the aft pull of the lowers resists the vang, which is trying to force the boom forwards. This results in less mast bend

On a reach, the vang pushes the boom into the mast, trying to bend the mast to windward. The leeward lower resists this

Adjustable Controls

Having set up the rig ashore, you can tweak the rig afloat using (in order of importance):

- Vang (kicking strap)
- Outhaul
- Cunningham
- Inhaul / tack adjustment
- Traveller / bridle system
- Centreboard
- Mainsheet tension

Vang (Kicking Strap)

To *windward* the vang:

1. Controls the leech profile of the mainsail, i.e. the twist. Pulling on the vang closes the leech, shown by the upper leech telltales starting to stall. Letting off the vang opens the leech and the telltales start to stream.

2. Pushes the boom forward on the mast, inducing fore-and-aft bend and flattening the mainsail. (Note that the mainsheet tension controls the leech *without* inducing mast bend.)

Offwind the only function of the vang is to control the leech. The sideways mast bend it causes is controlled by the lowers (if you have them).

On a reach the leech telltales must not be stalling, so ease the vang until they fly. This also straightens the mast, increasing power. Don't over-ease but, if in doubt, ease more!

On a run, ease the vang until the top 25% of the main is square to the wind to maximise the projected area. Don't let the top of the sail go further forward of abeam or you'll risk a death roll. Capsizing is always slow! However, in a singlehander without shrouds you may let out the boom to aid sailing by the lee (which is fast).

Pull on the kicker (and push down the centreboard) before gybing in light or medium winds to get the full effect from the roll gybe.

The leech telltales show how open the leech is
On a beat: stalling indicates it is too tight (top)
On a beat: streaming indicates it is too open (bottom)
Aim for streaming 40-60% of the time

Leech too open

Leech correct

Leech too closed

Leech too open

Leech correct

Leech too closed

Outhaul

Outhaul eased slightly for medium airs

Outhaul eased too much – the mainsail is too full in the lower batten area

Outhaul is too tight and too flat around the lower batten area

The outhaul is an underestimated control. In fact, it's a very powerful tool. **Use it to power up or depower the mainsail:**

- In light winds tighten the outhaul to flatten the lower part of the mainsail (not bar tight).
- In medium winds release it so that the clew moves forward about 25-40 mm. This powers up the mainsail and tightens the lower leech which helps pointing – ideal off the start line.
- As the wind increases pull the outhaul tight to flatten the lower sail and straighten the lower leech exit. A ridge forms along the foot, eliminating the sail's lens foot.

Note that in some classes, like the Phantom, the lower batten can invert in strong winds. So you may need to let off the outhaul to put more depth into the lower sail to eliminate this.

Cunningham

The cunningham controls the draft position in the mainsail. Pulling on the cunningham pulls the draft forward.

The cunningham also opens the top of the leech, because it bends the mast.

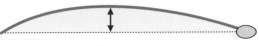

Force 1-2: with fine luff entry

Force2-3: with fuller sail

Force 4-6: cunningham applied to move the flow forwards

In light winds the cunningham should be right off, giving a flat entry. Don't worry about the creases behind the luff – they're fast!

Only pull on the control when you are overpowered. As the wind builds more, pull the cunningham **very** tight.

The cunningham is also very useful on a windy tight reach. Pull it on to flatten the head of the main and open the leech. Let the vang off a bit, raise the centreboard, and off you go!

> **TOP TIP**
>
> On an old sail the bolt rope may have shrunk, forcing you always to use cunningham tension. To cure the problem, undo the restraining stitching at the bottom end of the bolt rope, allowing it to slide up the tube of cloth in the sail. That's why there is a tail of bolt rope hanging down!

505 (from below):

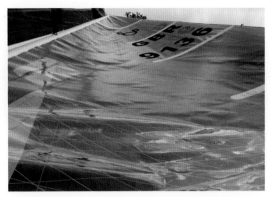

Very light air settings showing slightly more bend in the lower section

Medium air settings

Cunningham too tight for light airs, with a big crease down the luff and the draft too far forward

505 (from above):

Medium air setting with correct mast bend for the sails

Lighter air setting with more mast bend

Heavy air setting

Too much cunningham, resulting in a big crease appearing in the middle part of the top batten

Far too much mast bend with lots of distortion creases coming from the luff of the sail

Solo:

Correct set up with a soft entry

Too much cunningham with the draft being pulled too far forward for the conditions

Too much mast bend for the medium conditions, giving a lack of power in the rig

Inhaul / Tack Adjustment

An adjustable tack can be quite a powerful tool to increase fullness in the lower part of the sail or to flatten it, so special attention is needed set it up for the wind conditions and to get the desired flow over the sail, particularly in singlehanders. It is less critical in high performance boats.

Ideally you should not use the tack pin supplied on the boom because it holds the tack down. The sail can either be attached round the mast with a fixed strop or an adjustable inhaul which will control the horizontal (fore and aft) position of the tack.

The vertical (up and down) alignment is largely controlled by the cunningham, but you can have a button or a tie under a button using a strop.

Tack too far forward, pulling the draft of the mainsail too far forward

Tack in the correct position

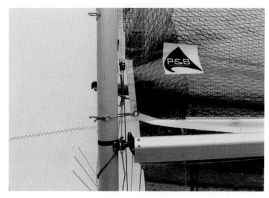

Tack too far back, making the sail entry too flat and meaning that the flow will be lost over the sail and the telltales will stall

Traveller / Bridle System
The traveller (or a bridle) is used to position the boom either side of the centreline.

In light to medium winds in a boat with a jib, when you're underpowered pull the traveller to windward so the boom is down the centreline. You may even need to raise it further to windward, so the leech of the sail is on the centreline.

Traveller system

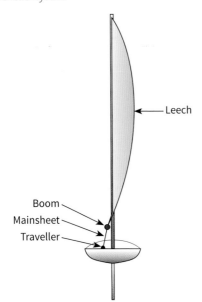

As the wind builds, lower the traveller and crank in the mainsheet. As the wind really gets up, let out the traveller a bit more, pull on the vang and play the mainsheet.

In a one-sailed boat you should always have the boom over the sidedeck or quarter to give some power. So use a combination of traveller, vang and mainsheet to achieve this – while keeping the leech tension you want.

Bridle system

If you have a bridle it should be adjusted for the current mast rake. The blocks should be almost touching, which means:
- The boom is on the centreline.
- You have to pull in less mainsheet when you want to pull in the mainsail.

Leech

Boom

Mainsheet

Traveller

Traveller and boom to windward. The leech begins on the centreline

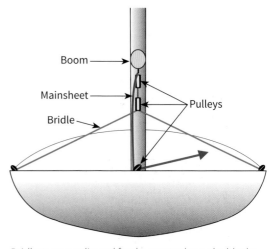

Boom

Mainsheet

Bridle

Pulleys

Bridle system adjusted for the mast rake so the blocks almost touch

Mainsail Controls: Summary

Different controls affect different parts of the mainsail.

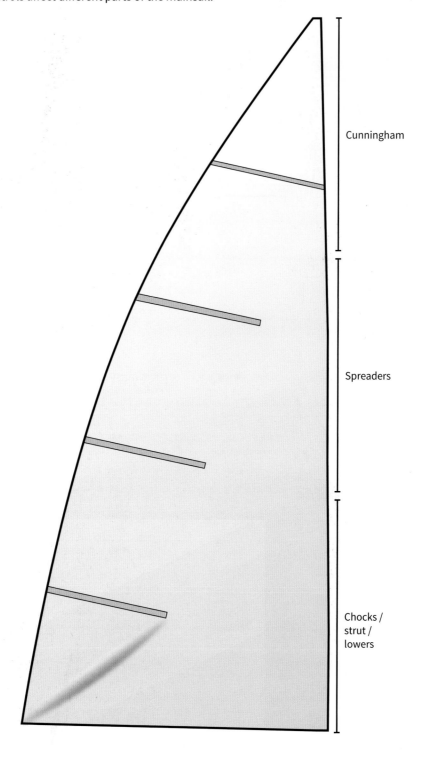

Cunningham

Spreaders

Chocks /
strut /
lowers

The Centreboard

The centreboard stops the boat slipping sideways, and also produces lift.

You can also raise it to depower, because the boat then slips a bit and 'rides with the punch'. Raising the board will help you turn without using too much rudder (which slows you down). For example, pull it up a bit before you bear away at the windward mark.

Since you should be continually altering the board's rake, you must have a system for adjusting it while you are hiking.

In light winds the board should be angled forwards, up to 15 degrees. The rig will have been raked more upright, so this puts the boat back in balance. It also gives the helm a bit more feel.

In medium winds the front edge should be vertical.

In strong winds the mast is raked back so raise the centreboard to balance the boat. Angling the board like this also reduces lift from the board, thus reducing heeling. It also stops the boat luffing up.

Have a system which allows you to adjust your board while hiking. On our 505 the downhaul is led back to the helm and the uphaul to the crew on the trapeze

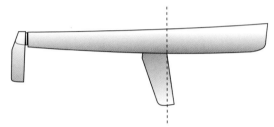

Light wind: board raked forward

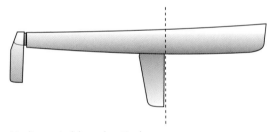

Medium wind: board vertical

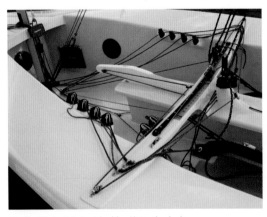

On the Solo it is just led back to the helm

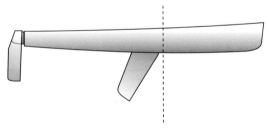

Strong wind: board raked aft to balance the boat and reduce heel

You need to calibrate the board, using a square edge near the front. You will finish up with three lines, depicting the light, medium and strong wind positions.

Calibrate your centreboard with light, medium and strong wind positions

Downwind you are going fast so need much less centreboard in the water. Indeed, going straight downwind you can try pulling it right up into the case. But lower a bit of board to form a skeg if the boat starts rolling!

Remember to put some board down before you gybe in light winds, to gain from the rolling effect. When gybing in hairy conditions have the board about half down.

Mainsheet Tension
The mainsheet controls the angle of attack of the mainsail to the breeze.

Mainsheet tension can also be used to power up the leech (it bends the upper mast a little). This can be an alternative to the vang, which also bends the lower mast.

Mainsheet tension too eased   *Mainsheet tension correct*   *Mainsheet tension too tight*

The Jib Controls

Many adjustments can be made to control the jib:
- Luff wire
- Stuff luff and lashings
- Jib cunningham
- Jib halyard
- Jibsheet angle
- Jibsheet tension

In addition you will use telltales to check that the jib is working properly.

Luff Wire

The jib has a stuff luff (a tube of cloth) at the luff and a luff wire which goes through it. The luff wire is part of the **standing rigging**, and you should use the same wire when you change jibs. (Many jibs now have luff zips to make this process easier.) Then your rake calibrations are the same whichever jib you use.

The jib halyard is attached to the top of the luff wire. The bottom of the luff wire is attached to an eye on the foredeck.

Stuff Luff & Lashings

The stuff luff slides over the luff wire. It is attached to the luff wire at the top by a lashing, which should be long enough that the head of the jib can twist naturally from one tack to the other.

The stuff luff is attached at the bottom by a lashing, or to the jib cunningham. These lashings are adjusted to give the correct draft position and to make the middle of the foot just touch the foredeck. This improves the airflow over both sides of the jib, shooting more wind onto the windward side and preventing air passing under the jib and destroying the low pressure on the leeward side.

Note that the forestay is irrelevant. It is just there to hold up the mast when the jib is lowered.

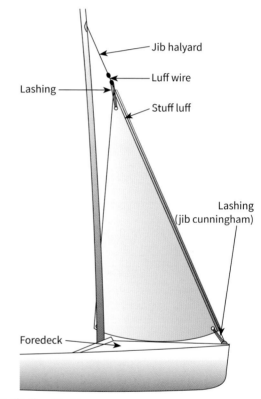

Stuff luff and lashings

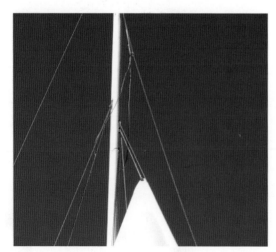

Stuff luff attachment at head of jib

Stuff luff attachment at bottom of jib

Jib Cunningham

The jib cunningham controls the flow in the jib. Tighten it in a breeze to pull the draft forward. In medium winds have a medium tension to give a smooth entry. In light winds loosen it so there is a hint of creasing behind the luff.

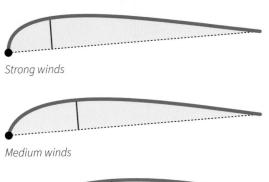

Strong winds

Medium winds

Light winds
The effect of the jib cunnigham

Jib Halyard

The jib halyard is pulled to give tension. If the tension is increased there is less sag in the stuff luff, giving the jib a flatter entry – which is good for strong winds. Less tension is used in medium air to give more luff round. (Note that to change the rake you adjust the jib halyard AND the shrouds).

Jibsheet Angle

Vertical Angle

The vertical angle of the jibsheet (in sync with the jibsheet tension) adjusts the shape of the jib. In the diagram (right):

- Jibsheet A is fairly horizontal. This gives a tight foot and an open leech, which are useful in light and strong winds.
- Jibsheet B is more vertical, giving a fuller sail and a tighter leech: this is a good setting for medium winds.
- Jibsheet C has an even tighter leech, good for pointing out of the start line, or in lighter winds and flat water.

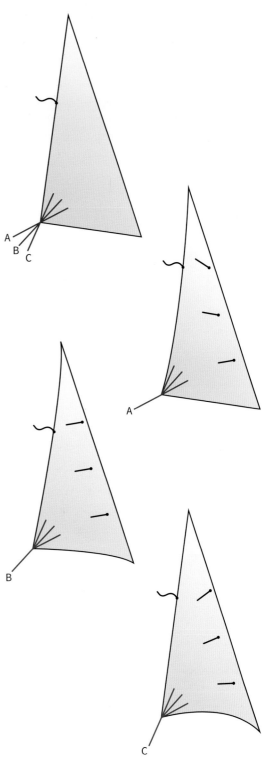

The effect of the vertical jibsheet angle on sail shape

Control of the vertical angle of the jibsheet is achieved in three different ways, dependent on class.

1. Clewboard (e.g. 49er, 29er)
The sheet lead is constant on the deck and the angle of the jibsheet is altered by attaching it to a different hole on the clewboard. You may need to change hole if the mast rake alters.

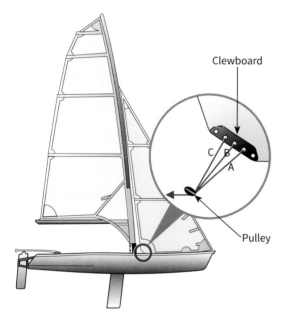

A clewboard on a 29er

2. Adjustable blocks (e.g. 505)

Adjustable blocks on jibsheet

3. Jib tracks (e.g. 2000)

Jib tracks

Whichever of the three methods is used, there should be sheeting lines marked on the jib so the crew can line up the jibsheet for the best angle.

Sheeting lines marked on the jib

Horizontal Angle

The horizontal (or inboard / outboard) sheeting angle of the jib to the centreline affects the slot between the mainsail and jib, and the pointing angle.

Move the sheeting angle inwards until the leading edge of the mainsail is almost backwinded. The idea is for the air to be slightly squeezed through the slot, which accelerates the air.

Note that you can sheet the jib closer if the mainsail is down the centreline and set with a flat entry. Close sheeting also means you can point higher.

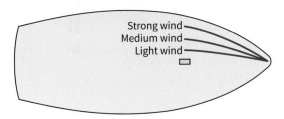

Sheeting angle relative to wind strength

Control of the horizontal angle of the jib is achieved in two different ways, dependent on class.

1. Jib track (e.g. 49er, 29er)

Jib track

2. Barber hauler (e.g. 505)

Barber hauler

On the 29er you would use the following settings for the clewboard (as shown opposite) and jib track:

Conditions	Clewboard	Jib track
Light winds & wavy	Bottom (A)	Inner pin setting
Medium winds, flat water	Top (C) or Middle (B)	Middle pin setting
Heavy winds, flat water	Bottom (A)	Outer pin setting
Heavy winds & wavy	Middle (B)	No pins (completely out)

On my 505, the horizontal control line is continuous, because the setting is the same on both tacks. But there are separate vertical controls on each side because the waves are seldom at right angles to the wind, meaning that you need a different setting on each tack.

Jibsheet Tension

The jibsheet tension also affects sheeting angle, sail shape and leech tension. Have bold marks on each jibsheet so that you can reproduce fast settings, and so the helmsman can see what's happening.

In fact all the control lines need to be calibrated so you can go through the gears easily.

The best way to attach the jibsheets is using a Q-lock – the same as you use at the tack of the mainsail. This is spliced to a thin rope. Adjust a knot in the rope to give the correct length of loop, then tape the Q-lock. The thin rope passes through an eye in the end of each jibsheet. Always tie the sheets in the same way so the calibration remains the same.

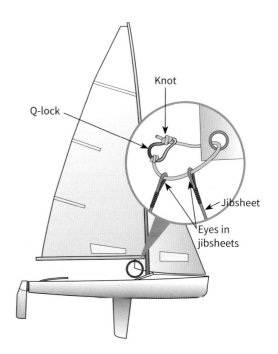

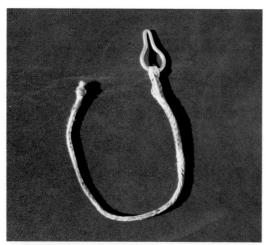

Q-lock

Attach jibsheets using a Q-lock

Jib Telltales

When the jib is set correctly all the luff telltales should break together as you luff. If they don't, adjust the fore-and-aft jib lead and the sheet tension until they do.

- If the top windward telltale is breaking first you have too much twist. Move the lead forward and / or sheet in.
- If the bottom windward telltale is breaking first you have too little twist. Move the lead aft and / or sheet out.

The leech telltale is even more important, and it is used for fine adjustment. There should be a window in the mainsail so that you can easily see the jib leech telltale:

- If it is streaming all the time the slot is too open.
- In light and strong winds it should be streaming most of the time.
- At the start it should stall, showing the jib leech is tight, for pointing.
- In medium winds the leech telltale should be breaking half the time.

What the jib leech telltales show:
A: Leech too tight
B: Correct for medium air
C: Correct for light and strong winds if streaming most (but not all) of the time

Jib luff telltales streaming together

Jib luff telltales not streaming together

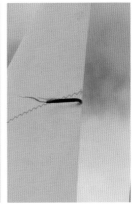

Jib leech telltales streaming all the time: slot too open

Jib leech telltales stalling all the time: leech too tight

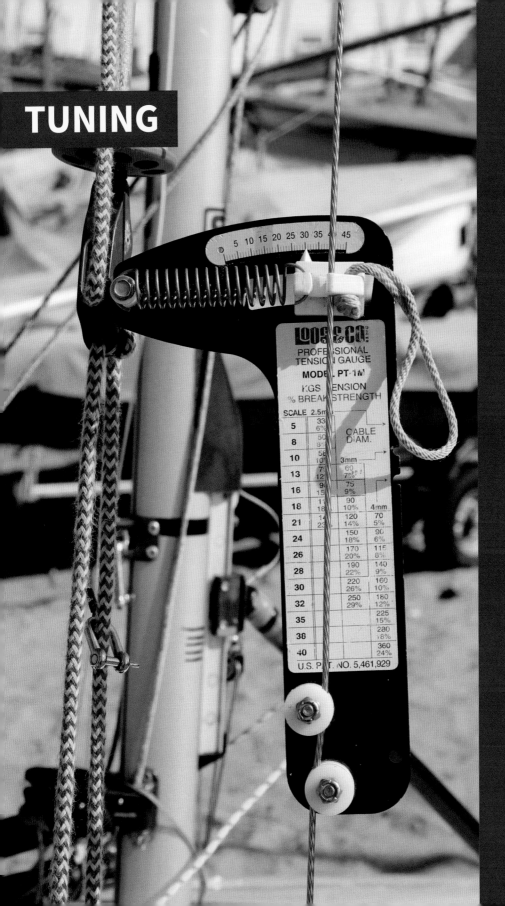

Loos&Co.®
PROFESSIONAL
TENSION GAUGE
MODEL PT-1M
KGS TENSION
% BREAK STRENGTH

SCALE	2.5mm		
5	33 6%	CABLE DIAM.	
8	50 8%		
10	58 10%	3mm	
13	70 12%	60 7%	
16	90 15%	75 9%	
18	110 18%	90 10%	4mm
21	140 23%	120 14%	70 5%
24		150 18%	90 6%
26		170 20%	115 8%
28		190 22%	140 9%
30		220 26%	160 10%
32		250 29%	180 12%
35			225 15%
38			280 18%
40			360 24%

U.S. PAT. NO. 5,461,929

PART 2

Preparing Your Boat

Step 1: Ask Your Sailmaker For A Tuning Guide

Your sailmaker should be able to give you a tuning guide with all the key numbers that you need. Here are P&B's current guides for the Solo and 505, but they are being updated all the time, so you are best checking for the latest versions at: www.pinbax.com/index.asp?selection=Tuning%20Guides

You can also check out fast boats in your class. But without the numbers it will take a long time to make your new boat fast!

Solo Tuning Guide

Sept 2016

The Solo is a relatively simple one-design class. With speed differences minimal and a boat that has little adjustment on the water, it is essential that the right rig settings are chosen before launching.

Mast foot position

The distance from the front of the mast, at the heel, to the outside of the transom should be 3060 mm.

Set up

Use your forestay and shrouds so that the mast sits as per the instructions below. The measurement is best achieved without the sail raised.

For a rough setting, push the mast to the back of the gate and adjust the forestay so that it is just under tension.

- First define your rake – pull a tape measure to the top of the mast and measure to the top of the gooseneck black band. The measurement for this is 5030 mm.
- Once you have achieved this measurement, take the tape to the transom. Check your rake measurement and move your forestay position until you reach 5960 mm.
- To set the shrouds, pull the mast forward at deck level, the mast should just touch the front of the gate.

Below is a simple chart to help you set up your boat once you have achieved the above.

	Light	Medium	Heavy
Forestay		– 1 hole (up)	2 holes (up)
Rake	5960 mm	5930 mm	5900 mm
Shrouds		+ ½ hole (down)	+ 1 hole (down)
Chocks	5 mm	10 mm	10-15 mm

Chocks

We supply 3 chocks. When a chock is not in use it should be placed behind the mast, so that it eliminates movement.

Centreboard

Turn the boat on its side and lower the board to find the vertical position. This is your datum point to work from so mark it clearly on the handle of the board. In very light conditions the board should be positioned forward of the vertical point and slowly raised as the wind increases and you begin to hike. With increasing wind raise the board beyond the vertical point to reduce the weather helm and depower the boat.

Traveller

Only in very light airs should the traveller be positioned in the centreline of the boat. With increasing wind ease from this position up to a maximum of 380 mm using the mainsheet tension to control the leech.

- Light airs: cleat 75-100 mm off the centreline
- Medium airs: cleat 100-150 mm off the centreline
- Heavy airs: cleat 150-380 mm off the centreline

Kicker

This should be set so the slack is just taken out of the system when the main is sheeted in. As the wind increases it can be used to depower the sail by bending the mast and flattening the sail. In heavy airs the kicker must be eased before you tack!

Outhaul

In very light winds the sail should be pulled out to the black band, in medium airs ease outhaul up to 60 mm from band. When overpowered pull sail out to black band upwind; to increase power downwind ease this up to 75 mm.

Cunningham

This is an effective way to depower the sail, flattening the sail and opening the leech. Use only to remove excess creases in medium conditions but pull hard to depower in heavy conditions.

505 Alto & M2 Tuning Guide

Wind Speed (knots)	0-4	4-8
Mast Rake	7900 mm	7900-7850 mm
Rig Tension Shrouds	32	30
Shroud Tracks	Forward 1 hole	2650 mm
Kicker	-	-
Reason	-	To stop boom skying when tacking or easing
Cunningham	No	No
Jib Fairleads from Centreline	400 mm	400-450 mm
Strut (from neutral-upright setting)	– 30 mm	– 10 mm
Jib Luff Tension	No creases	See creases
Centreboard Position	10° forward in gybe	10° forward in gybe
Outhaul	Tight	Ease 15 mm

Spreaders
Mast should have 5 mm prebend
@ 7850 mm rake
Shrouds 1 hole back neutral

Mast
Foot 3060 mm from station 11
Shroud from transom 2650 mm (neutral)
Mast rake measure from top band on mount to inside floor transom

Sept 2016

A 130-145 mm   **B** 390-420 mm crew weight dependent

8-12	12-17	17-22	22 +
7850-7760 mm	7760-7650 mm	7650-7500 mm	7450 mm
30	30	32	33
Aft 1 hole	Aft 1 hole	Aft 2 holes	Aft 2 holes +
A bit	Yes	Loads	Loads
To control twist	To control twist	To control twist & bend mast	To bend mast & flatten mainsail
No	No	Yes	Yes
450-520 mm	520-570 mm	570-610 mm	610-680 mm
0	+ 10-20 mm	+ 20-25 mm	+ 25-30 mm
Just a hint of creases	No creases	Tension (a little)	Tension (a little)
Straight down in gybe	Raise 2-6 cm In choppy water: raise more	Raise 7-10 cm In choppy water: raise more	Raise 11-15 cm
Ease 10 mm	Tight	Very tight	Very tight

Step 2: Getting The Hull Right

The mast step and gate go in first. Check the class rules, the tuning guide and the design plan of the boat (get this from the designer).

Use a spirit level to get the boat horizontal. Position the mast step in the centre of the boat. Then use a laser to get the mast step and gate in line. If you don't have a laser, use the process described below.

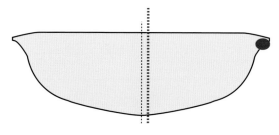

Too much filler on the right means the central point will be to the right of the centre line

Use a laser to set the mast step and gate in line

TOP TIP

Have a good look at the deck-hull join. Is it symmetrical all the way round the gunwale? If the filler is thicker on one side than the other, the boat isn't symmetrical and you will have to allow for this when you site the mast gate and shroud plates.

In the diagram (top right), the hull / deck joint is thicker on the right, so siting the mast step halfway will put it to the right of the centre line. In this case, use a string from the bow to the centre of the transom and site the mast step directly beneath the string.

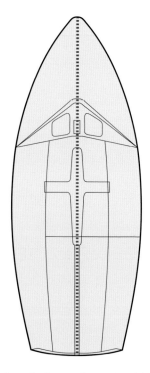

Use a string from the bow to the centre of the transom to find the centre line

Having established this fundamental line, you can now work outwards to position the shrouds and bow fitting – in other words the fore triangle will be symmetrical. This is vital to ensure that the mast is vertical sideways in the boat.

The diagram opposite shows how this works. **A** is the bow fitting. **B** is the middle of the mast gate. **C**-**C**^{1} are parallel lines equidistant from **B**. Finally, make two equal arcs **D** to establish the shroud bases (**E**).

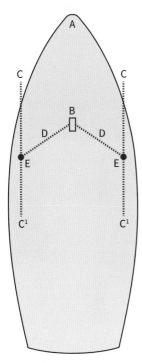

How to position the shroud and bow fittings

Line up the bottom pintle with the centreboard using a laser

Step 3: Check The Foils

Note that heavy crews should choose a stiff centreboard. Lighter crews should have a softer board, which will depower in a gust.

Turn the boat upside down and push the board down. Measure from the tip to the gunwale each side to make sure the board is vertical. If necessary pack one side, inside the case, until it **is** vertical.

The board should fit snugly in the case but still go up and down. You can stick low friction tape on it to make adjusting it easier. The quicker you can move the centreboard the quicker you can go through the gears.

The next job is to align the rudder with the centreboard, which is really important for speed downwind. (Even if the centreboard is slightly out of alignment, align the rudder with it.) With the boat the right way up, bolt on the bottom pintle. Then invert the boat, fit the rudder and use a laser to align it with to centreboard. (If you don't have a laser you will have to do this by eye.) Attach the top pintle in this position.

Rudder and centreboard aligned for maximum speed

Rudder and centreboard not aligned will slow you down

Step 4: Set Up the Spreaders

Fit the spreaders onto the mast according to the tuning guide.

Put a batten across the shroud base and another batten across the spreader tips. Sight down the mast: the two battens should be parallel, showing that the spreaders have been fitted symmetrically.

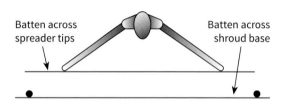

If the spreaders have been fitted symmetrically, the two battens will be parallel

If they have not been fitted symmetrically, adjust the spreaders so that they make the mast bend evenly from one tack to the other.

Step 5: Set Up the Mast

Check that the shrouds are the same length (if not, get new ones which are), then fit them. (Note that they will stretch a bit initially, then they'll stay put.)

Now fit the mast into the boat. Check that it's a snug fit sideways in the mast gate. If it isn't, pad the gate with either Jap tape or an old credit card.

The mast should fit snugly in the mast gate

Pull on the rig tension and eyeball up the back of the mast. It should be straight sideways. If not:
- The shroud bases are asymmetric, or
- The spreaders are not symmetrical, or
- The mast step is not central.

Check and rectify.

The Initial Set-Up

The boat is set up initially for beating in light airs. Later, you will modify this for medium and strong winds.

We now want to set the correct rake, pre-bend and rig tension for light airs.

Step 1: Set The Mast Rake

The rake is measured with a tape measure from the bottom of the upper black band on the mast, to a point on the transom defined in the tuning guide.

Pull on the rig tension for light airs according to the tuning guide. Attach a tape measure to the main halyard and hoist it fully. Run the tape measure down the mast and take a reading at the top of the gooseneck black band. The reading should be the same as the distance between the bands – on a Solo, for example, this is 5030 mm (1).

Adjust the halyard until the reading on the tape measure is 5030 mm. This shows that the tape measure is hoisted to the correct height. Finally, maintain the same pressure on the tape measure and swing it to the designated point on the transom and measure the distance from the upper black band. This reading is your rake.

The tuning guide says the rake should be:
- Light wind 5960 mm
- Medium wind 5930 mm
- Strong wind 5900 mm

So adjust the rake until you get 5960 mm (2). (Note that the smaller the measurement, the larger the rake.)

(If this is too technical, launch the boat and hang a weight on the main halyard. Measure from the halyard to the gooseneck black band to get an idea of rake. Maybe start with 300 mm and see how you go.)

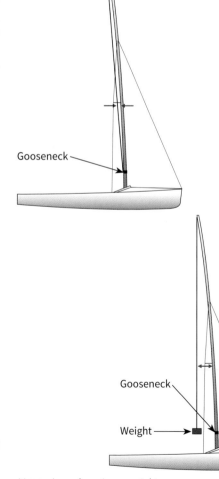

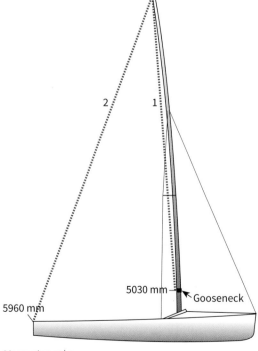

Measuring rake

Measuring rake using a weight

Step 2: Set The Pre-Bend & Rig Tension

Now check the pre-bend. This is measured at spreader height, with no sail up.

Pull the halyard down to the bottom black band and measure the distance from the track to the halyard at spreader height. This is the pre-bend. The tuning guide will specify what you need, so rake the spreaders until you get the right value. (Rake the spreaders aft to increase the pre-bend, and forward to decrease it.) If you don't have a tuning guide, initially try something between 20 and 35 mm.

The diagram (right) and photo (below) show a useful gadget for measuring pre-bend. Slide it up the mast track to spreader height (you may need to stand on the boom), stretch the halyard as described above, and read off the pre-bend.

Without pre-bend the mainsail would be far too full behind the luff in light winds. The more flexible the mast, the more pre-bend you need.

Setting your boat up to give pre-bend in the mast obviously means your rig is in tension. This is what you want for sailing, but it isn't good for the hull, particularly if it is fairly flexible, like a 29er. Once you have finished sailing, make sure you let the tension off and then put the tension back on before your next outing. Using a 'boat breaker' is an effective way of doing this.

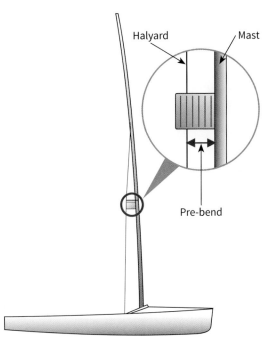

Pre-bend and how to measure it

Gadget for measuring pre-bend

Use a 'boat breaker' with a high purchase to take off and put on the required rig tension

Step 3: Checking & Adjusting The Settings

Finally, check that the rake, rig tension and pre-bend are all as specified in the tuning guide. If not, fiddle around with them until they are all spot on. Your rig is now set up for light winds!

Of course, you will need to adjust the rake for different wind strengths. Note that, because of the geometry of the shrouds and jib halyard / forestay, the jib halyard / forestay setting moves more than the shroud settings. You might, for example, need to rake the mast back by lengthening the jib halyard / forestay a 'whole hole', but you will only need to tighten each shroud by 'half a hole' to maintain the rig tension.

Some classes prohibit systems for adjusting the shrouds while racing. If your class has this rule, remember that the rake is more important than the rig tension. In the Solo, for example, if the wind pipes up between races you need to move forward and pull out the fast pin in the forestay adjuster. You can't adjust the shrouds, so the mast rakes back at the expense of rig tension. On balance this is faster than making no adjustment. The same is true in the 470 and Fireball classes. The 505 allows shroud adjusters so you can let off the jib halyard and tighten the shrouds in sync.

De-raker plate and shroud adjuster

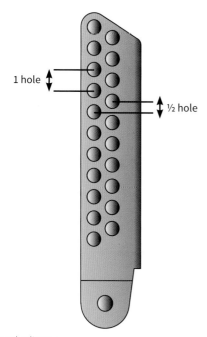

1 hole

½ hole

Shroud adjuster

A fast pin with a de-raker allows for speedy adjustment on the water. The bottom shroud is attached to a stainless steel plate with two slots – one for the fixed pin at the top of the forestay adjuster and one for the fast pin. This means that, when you release the fast pin, the forestay is still attached and you don't lose your rig completely! Go afloat with the fast pin in place and (if necessary) pull it out before the start to change the rake.

Fixed pin

Fast pin

Shroud adjuster with fast pin

Step 4: Have A Look At The Mainsail

Pull up the mainsail and adjust the cunningham, outhaul and vang for light airs.

Sight up the mainsail, or lay a batten horizontally from the luff to the leech to show where the draft is. At mid-height the maximum draft should be ⅓ back from the mast. The diagram below shows what you're looking for.

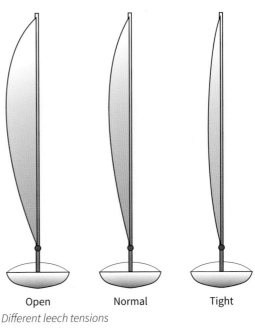

Open   Normal   Tight

Different leech tensions

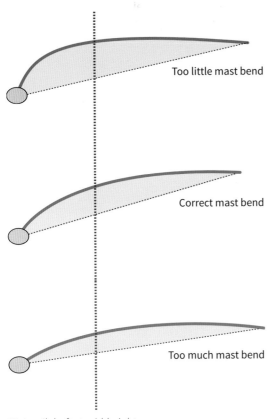

Too little mast bend

Correct mast bend

Too much mast bend

Mainsail draft at mid-height

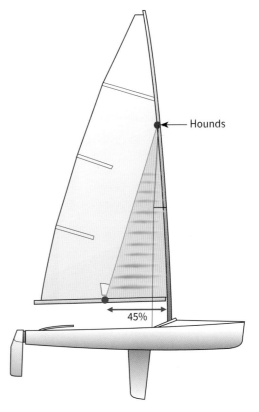

Hounds

45%

Look from astern to see how open the leech is (above right).

With the cunningham slack, you should have creases running from the mast to a line from the hounds to 45% of the way aft along the boom. If the creases don't do this, adjust the spreaders, chocks and lowers until they do. **Speed creases are fast**, and it's definitely fastest if this whole triangle is filled with creases. (But do avoid the creases going more than 50% aft.)

With the cunningham slack you should have creases in this area

Step 5: Check The Slot

Put up the jib and look at the slot (between the mainsail and jib). The leech of the jib should be parallel with the nearest bit of the mainsail (maybe a little closer at the top). Adjust the jibsheet fairlead to achieve this.

Slot too closed   *Slot correct for medium airs*   *Slot too open*

Step 6: Calibration

Calibrate all the control lines and record the settings you established in *Preparing Your Boat* Steps 1-5 and *The Initial Set-Up* Steps 1-5. For example, put a mark on the cascade vang system, and see how one of the blocks moves against this line.

Calibrate all your control lines & fittings and record the settings

Note that we have tuned for upwind. Don't worry about offwind tuning at this stage – you simply want the mainsail to be as full as possible downwind. Pre-bend, for example, doesn't come into it because the pre-bend is fore and aft. With the boom out you would need sideways pre-bend to affect the fullness!

Refining The Set-Up

In the previous section we set up the boat for light winds, say 4-10 knots, which is the basis for tuning. Now we will modify those settings for beating in other wind strengths.

Super-Light Wind Settings

If the wind is only 0-4 knots you need flatter sails with more twist, to encourage the feeble breeze to flow round the sails. Bending the mast to flatten the mainsail is a key element.

Equipment / control	What to do in **super-light wind**	Reason
Sails	Use your flattest	To allow the wind to flow
Rake: Jib halyard / forestay	Same as for light air	
Rig tension: Shrouds	Tighten shrouds to increase rig tension	To bend the mast and flatten the mainsail
Spreaders / shroud base	Rake the spreaders aft, or move the shroud tracks forward	To induce pre-bend
Mast gate / strut	Remove chocks from in front of mast and back chock putting them behind the mast. Or wind the strut forward	To give some low mast bend
Lowers	Loosen	To help the mast bend forwards
Vang	Off (take up slack so the boom doesn't sky when you tack)	To allow twist
Outhaul	Very tight	To flatten the sail as much as possible
Cunningham	Off (don't worry about creases behind the luff)	To give a flat entry
Traveller & mainsheet	Arrange the traveller to windward so that, with no mainsheet tension, the boom is down the centreline. For one-sail boats have the boom on the quarter	To keep the slot open
Centreboard	Same as for light winds – raked forwards	
Telltales	Useless!	
Jib cunningham	Off, to give a hint of creasing at the luff	To keep the entry fine, otherwise the fullness is pulled too far forward
Jib leads	Move the leads outwards Move the leads aft or up	To open the slot To twist the leech
Jibsheet	Ease	To open the slot and twist the leech

Medium Wind Settings (Trapezing)

If the wind is 10-16 knots you are aiming to power up the rig. This means more fullness in the sails, and straight leeches. Remember, the initial setup was for light winds. We now need to modify the rig for medium airs.

Equipment / control	What to do in **medium wind**	Reason
Sails	Use your full sails and big spinnaker	To get maximum power
Rake: Jib halyard / forestay	Increase the rake – typically by slackening the jib halyard / forestay by 1 unit and tightening the shrouds by ½ unit	Nobody knows why, but rake works!
Rig tension: Shrouds	Keep the same by adjusting jib halyard / forestay and shrouds in sync	
Spreaders / shroud base	Rake the spreaders forward, or move the shroud tracks aft	To straighten the mast
Mast gate / strut	Chock fully (or wind on the strut)	To straighten the mast
Lowers	Maximum tightness	To straighten the mast
Vang	Pull on so that upper leech telltales are streaming 60-70% of the time	To close the leech
Outhaul	Ease 3-5 cm	To make the main fuller
Cunningham	Off	To get maximum power
Traveller & mainsheet	Pull on mainsheet. Adjust the traveller so the boom is down the centreline	To power up the main and set the leech
Centreboard	Vertical	
Telltales	Upper leech telltale should be streaming 60-70% of the time	
Jib cunningham	Pull on a bit	To give a smooth entry
Jib leads	Move inboard	To narrow the slot and give you more power
	Move forward or down	To tighten the leech
Jibsheet	Pull so leech is parallel to nearest part of the main. Watch the top leech telltale on the jib – should be falling away about 30% of the time	To create a good slot

Strong Wind Settings (Depowering)

If the wind is over 16 knots your aim is to depower. This is achieved by flattening the sails, inducing more twist and reducing backwinding.

Equipment / control	What to do in **strong wind**	Reason
Sails	Use your flat sails and small spinnaker	To give less drag and increase boatspeed via flatness and open leeches

Equipment / control	What to do in **strong wind**	Reason
Battens	Put in stiff battens	To flatten the leech exit
Rake: Jib halyard / forestay	Let off halyard / forestay to strong wind setting to increase rake	To lower centre of effort, reducing heeling, and move centre of effort aft to allow you to raise the centreboard
Rig tension: Shrouds	High tension	To keep the jib luff straight
Spreaders / shroud base	Angle spreaders forward or move shroud tracks aft	To compensate for increased rake
Mast gate / strut	Add chocks in front of mast (wind the strut aft)	To keep some tension on the lower leech
Lowers	Ease slightly	To allow the mast to bend
Vang	Pull on hard. In a gust, dump the mainsheet (and the jibsheet too, if necessary)	To control the mainsail
Outhaul	Pull on hard, even to the maximum	To flatten the sail
Cunningham	Pull on tight	To depower and keep the flow forward
Traveller & mainsheet	Ease the traveller. With the vang tight, play the mainsheet	To keep the boom on the quarter and the boat flat
Centreboard	Raise a lot and even more in waves (two more numbers on calibration strip). If you have a daggerboard, raise it a bit	Since you are footing you will go faster and need less board: you are, in effect, reaching to windward
Telltales	Streaming all the time, so useless for tuning	
Jib cunningham	On hard	To pull the draft forward
Jib leads	Move outboard Move aft or up	To open the slot To slacken the leech
Jibsheet	Pull tight (gauge by watching the jib leech telltales). Ease in big gusts, as the main goes out	To control twist

Offwind Settings

Having concentrated so far on beating, I will now go through how this changes for offwind sailing.

Reaching In Light & Medium Air

First of all, let's look at how to modify the rig for reaching, compared with beating in the same wind strength. In other words, this is what you should do as you round the windward mark onto a reach.

The objective for light and medium air reaching is maximum power, achieved by staightening the mast fore and aft and sideways. The most important controls on a reach are the sheets, vang and outhaul.

The following controls can be ignored, i.e. the settings are the same as they were on the beat:
- Choice of sails
- Spreaders (and shroud base adjusters)
- Mast gate
- Traveller
- Jib cunningham

The ones which may need tweaking are:

Jib Halyard & Shrouds

For most classes these stay put. But for a non-spinnaker boat it pays to let off the leeward shroud, allowing the mast to straighten.

Lowers

Pull on the lowers. This straightens the mast, powering up the mainsail.

Vang

The vang controls the mainsail's leech. The leech should have a gradual twist. Ease the vang until the mainsail's top leech telltale is streaming all the time (never stalling). This helps straighten the mast and powers up the rig.

Outhaul

Ease the outhaul to give a full lens foot.

Cunningham

Off.

Centreboard

Push up until you have about half board.

Telltales

Use the middle luff telltales on the main. These should be streaming all the time, but if in doubt let out the mainsheet a bit – out too far is less damaging than in too tight.

Jib Leads

On a reach, the problem is that the jib twists too much. To prevent this barber-haul the jibsheet outboard, or move the fairleads forward. Inevitably there will be some twist, so trim to the middle jib luff telltale which should be streaming both sides.

Spinnaker

The boom and the spinnaker pole should always be in line. Set the pole height so that the clews are level. The pole will be higher as the wind increases.

In really light airs, roll up the jib (if possible). Lower the pole and sail high to try to fill the sail. If this doesn't work, drop the kite. It is only causing drag.

Reaching In Strong Winds

As the wind builds you need to tweak some more.

Vang

Let off the vang rather more. The twist depowers the main and reduces backwinding.

In spinnaker boats you often need to dump the vang completely to depower the main and keep the boom out of the water. You are essentially sailing on the spinnaker.

Outhaul

The outhaul is eased until you can no longer cope with the power. Then gradually tighten it.

Cunningham

Pulling on the cunningham depowers the main. In spinnaker boats pull it on hard, i.e. cunningham on, vang off.

Centreboard

Raise more than halfway. You're going fast so don't need much sideways resistance.

Spinnaker

If the reach is tight lower the pole. This also helps depower the kite in really strong winds.

Ease the spinnaker sheet so the kite's leading edge is really on the curl. Ensure you keep it there!

Running In Light & Medium Air

This section covers running in light and medium air, compared with beating in the same wind strengths. In other words, this is what you should do as you round the windward mark onto a run.

Your objectives are to maximise speed, but also to make progress to leeward. Achieve them by heading up to go faster, which increases the apparent wind. Then use the speed to head down.

Your course is very class dependent. In a 470 you can sail almost straight downwind. In a 505 and an asymmetric boat you reach downwind with the crew on the trapeze, keeping the speed up so the apparent wind goes forward.

The course is also dependent on crew weight: heavy crews need to go higher.

The following controls can be ignored, as the settings are the same as they were for the beat:
- Spreaders and shroud base
- Mast gate
- Traveller
- Jib cunningham

The ones you need to tweak are:

Jib Halyard & Shrouds
Let off the shrouds so the mast is raked upright or even forward. (Compared to aft rake, this gives more projected area. And in light winds raking forward will help raise the stern, reducing skin friction.) Then tighten the jib halyard / forestay to keep the rig tension.

Lowers
Ease the lowers to allow the mast to rake forward.

Vang
Ease right off until the top part of the main is at right angles to the breeze.

However, with an unstayed rig you can keep the vang on, let out the sheet, bear away and reverse the air flow by running by the lee.

Outhaul
Pull right out to maximise the projected area of the main.

Cunningham

Right off.

Centreboard

Raise 80-90%. But put some board down to gybe.

Telltales

The mainsail's top leech telltale should be streaming.

Jibsheet

On a non-spinnaker boat, goosewing the jib using a hand. If you have a whisker pole, set it, and tighten the jibsheet to stop the upper leech of the jib twisting off.

On a spinnaker boat the helm sits to leeward, holding out the boom and using the same hand to hold up the spinnaker sheet. The crew is to windward. The crew lowers the pole, then trims the sheet and tells the helm when he needs to luff or when he can bear away.

Running In Strong Winds

Your objectives are to go fast but stay upright!

Most settings are the same as for running in light / medium air. Here are the exceptions:

Vang

Let off a bit of vang before you round the windward mark. This keeps the boom out of the water and helps you turn. Don't let off too much or you will fall in to windward.

Centreboard

Have about half the board in the water. This stabilises the boat – and gives you something to hang on to if you take a dive.

Spinnaker

In extreme conditions, pull on *both* twinning lines to stabilise the kite.

Spinnakers

In the previous sections I referred briefly to the spinnaker in different downwind conditions, but here I will discuss them in a bit more detail – both the symmetric and asymmetric variety.

Symmetric Spinnakers

The Gear

If class rules allow, you should have two spinnakers: a smaller flat one and a bigger full one.

(Note, in passing, that a spinnaker has two clews, because it can be set with either attached to the pole.)

For strong winds the sail is cut with a smaller half height. (To find the half height, fold the spinnaker as shown to find the centre of the clews, then measure across the sail.) It can still be reasonably full, and is generally faster reaching. If you are going to have lots of reaches (e.g. on a triangular course), or expect a blow, use this one.

For light winds you want the biggest sail you can get. This will be cut fuller, to hold out the shoulders. It is generally faster running, and is ideal for windward / leeward courses.

Site the sheave in the mast for the spinnaker halyard as high as the rules allow – you want maximum projected area. But have a knot with a bobble so that the kite flies 6-8 cm from the sheave – this keeps the head away from the mainsail. You can lead the halyard straight back to its cleat, or have a 1:2 system, where a small hard pull results in the sail shooting up.

Site the pole / mast attachment so that the pole is horizontal in average conditions, with the clews level – once again this gives the maximum projected area.

Tie each sheet to its clew so that they hold the sail close to the pole. If there is any slack the sail becomes unstable when flying.

Push the sheet through the grommet. Tie a thumb knot in the end of the sheet, then make a half hitch.

If you have them, twinning lines are positioned just in front of the shrouds. They pull down on the guy and control the pole.

You may need a prodder to prevent the sheets falling over the bow as you lower the spinnaker. Wrapping the kite round the centreboard is definitely slow!

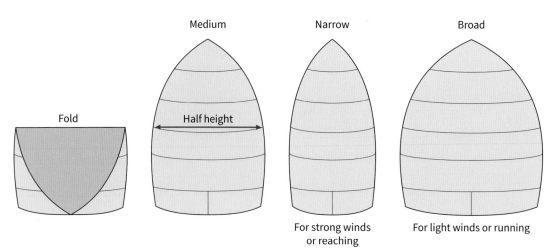

Medium   Narrow   Broad

Fold   Half height

For strong winds or reaching   For light winds or running

Measuring and looking at the half height

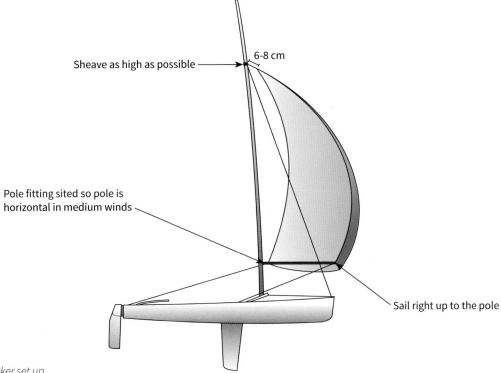

Sheave as high as possible

6-8 cm

Pole fitting sited so pole is
horizontal in medium winds

Sail right up to the pole

Spinnaker set up

Attach the lines to the clew with a half hitch on itself

Have a bobble so the kite flies 6-8 cm from the sheave   *A prodder prevents the sheets falling over the bow*

You may also want to have tags to stop the spinnaker sheet falling over the side into the water.

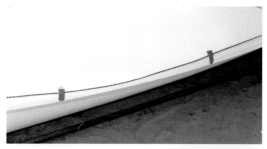

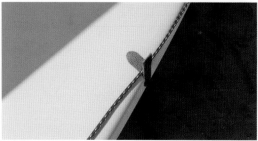

Tags can be put on the side of the foredeck to prevent the sheet going over the side

Whether you choose bags or a chute is a matter of preference (and class rules). In expert hands, bags are usually quicker, but a windward hoist is tricky. A chute is harder on the spinnaker and the crew has to do everything in the right order to prevent the sheets and retrieval line fouling up. If you're going for the chute option, coat the spinnaker with McLube SailKote when new to keep it slippery.

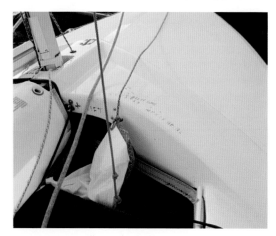

Bags are generally quicker to hoist...

Spinnaker Controls
The main controls are:
- Pole height
- Sheet (leeward) and guy (windward)
- Twinning lines
- Halyard

Pole Height
In general, fly the kite with the clews level. We have already seen that a horizontal pole has been set to achieve this for medium winds. In lighter air the unsupported clew droops so you will need to lower the pole to get the clews level. In strong winds you also may need to lower the pole to stabilise the boat and depower the spinnaker.

Sheet & Guy
Use the guy to set the pole square to the wind. As a rough check, the pole and boom should be in line. For speed you want to square the pole as much as the sail will allow.

Keep playing the sheet so the windward leech (the luff on a conventional sail) is beginning to curl – this shows the sail is as far out as possible without collapsing, which is what you want with any sail.

... but chutes are easier for windward hoists

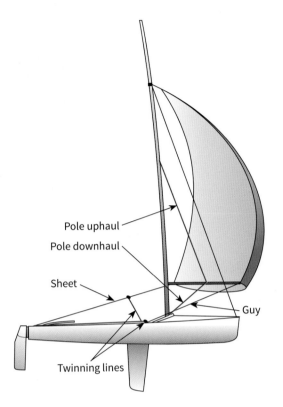

Pole uphaul
Pole downhaul
Sheet
Guy
Twinning lines

Spinnaker controls

On a reach the sheet leads should be as far aft as possible. (Of course, the twinning line pulls the guy down and forward.)

On a run, particularly in strong winds, it may be better to pull on both twinning lines to pull the leads forward, stabilising the kite.

Twinning Lines
These are used to control the lead of the sheet and guy. As you pull on a twinning line the lead effectively moves down and forward. Of course, the windward twinner is pulled tight to prevent the pole from skying, and to give the crew room to move outboard.

Halyard
Hoist to the bobble.

The spinnaker pole and boom should be in line

Asymmetric Spinnakers

In theory (!) the asymmetric is a simple sail with less to worry about in terms of both gear and controls than a symmetrical kite.

The Gear

Tie the tack with a bobble so the tack is about 10 cm away from the pole. In lighter airs, have the tack slightly further away from the pole to fill out the luff and kite (lean) the boat to windward to help rotate the spinnaker and give more projected area. When it's really windy, pull the tack down to tighten the luff.

In lighter airs have the tack away from the pole to fill out the luff and help rotate the spinnaker to windward

Because the clew needs to pass round the forestay when you gybe you need to attach the sheet to the clew without having any knots to catch or snag. Create a special soft loop from the core of the rope and then thread this through the clew eye and then thread the spinnaker sheets through this loop.

As with a symmetrical spinnaker, site the sheave in the mast for the spinnaker halyard as high as the rules allow – you want maximum projected area. Again use a bobble at the top of the halyard to prevent the sail being wound into the sheave, but you want the head of the sail close to it – you don't want the head to fall off to leeward of the mainsail.

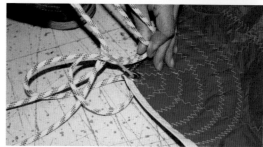

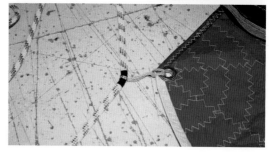

Attaching the sheet to the clew

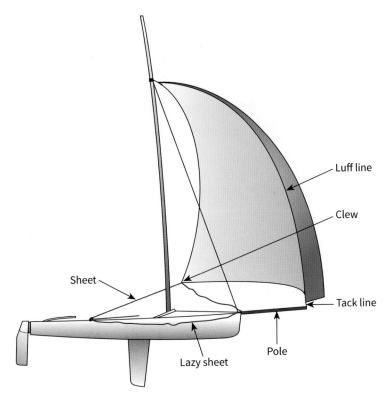

Asymmetric spinnaker set up

Asymmetric Spinnaker Controls

The controls are:

- Halyard
- Sheets
- Tack line
- Luff line

Halyard

Hoist the sail almost right up in most winds.

In super-light airs ease the halyard to keep the kite away from the main and allow some airflow between the two sails.

Sheets

The windward sheet (the lazy sheet) does nothing. (Note it's led to windward of the forestay!)

Play the leeward sheet to keep the luff on the curl.

Tack Line

This is usually set before you go sailing. Pull it tight in a breeze to flatten the kite. Ease off slightly in light airs.

Luff Line

This is a thin rope which runs inside the luff. It acts like a little cunningham, so pull it on in strong winds to pull the flow forward. This means the luff can curl more without collapsing, enabling the crew to ease more than usual.

A well designed spinnaker enables you to curl the spinnaker up to 600 mm, depowering it so that you can sail higher. This also helps the boat to stay upright.

Two Boat Tuning

If you follow the advice given so far, you should be fast. But if you want to go faster still you need to do some two boat tuning.

Choose a buddy who has the same (or similar) gear to you. Calibrate each boat the same, so that you can check each other's settings.

Set up both boats the same and beat for a few minutes in the position shown. (You need to sail close together so that you are in the same wind, but be far enough apart that you can steer round waves. The bow of the windward boat should be level with the mast of the leeward boat, and you should be about one and a half boat lengths apart.)

The idea is that you sail for a few minutes and see who is faster. Compare notes, then get the slower boat up to speed by getting her to **alter one thing at a time**. After each alteration, beat again to check if the change has worked. If it has, you can both adopt it. Then the slower boat makes another change, and so on. It's a time consuming process, but is the only real way to make progress.

It's even better if you have a coach in a coach boat, because an experienced person can see a lot from there. You should also try getting into the coach

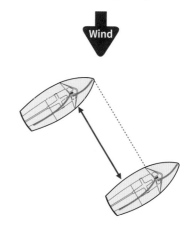

Two boat tuning positions upwind

Two boat tuning upwind

boat and watch while someone else sails your boat – you'll learn more from the RIB than from sailing your boat!

If you are confused about what to change, the slower boat might try changing:

- Rake
- Rig tension
- Mast gate control
- Jib lead position
- Centreboard rake

As you reach or run back downwind, you can do some two boat tuning too. On a reach, the following boat gets just ahead of the wake line (or she will shoot forward on it, giving you a false impression of speed). On a run the boats can be side by side.

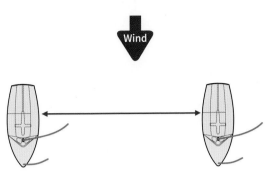

Two boat tuning positions on a run

Two boat tuning on a run

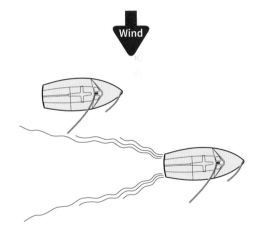

Two boat tuning positions on a reach

Two boat tuning on a reach

In short:

- **Identify the problem**
- **Alter something, making a subtle adjustment**

Remember, *overall* you are looking for a 2% increase in speed. You will seldom lose a race by more than that. Tuning has to be precise!

Once you and your buddy are fully up to speed (and are probably going the same speed) it's time to go racing!

Hopefully you will both be up the front, and can enjoy this reward for all your hard work. But if, for some reason, you are off the pace, help is at hand in the next chapter.

Troubleshooting

Despite your best efforts, you may find that you're slow in certain conditions. I hope the following will help you get back on track.

Common Problems

The possibilities are:
1. You point ok but are slow
2. You can't point, but are fast
3. You are low *and* slow
4. You are slow on the reach
5. You are slow on the run
6. You have trouble starting
7. You set up the rig for light airs but the wind has increased
8. You set up the rig for heavy air but the wind has dropped
9. You are slow in chop
10. You are slow in waves
11. You are slow in gusty winds

1. You point ok but are slow

This is probably caused by the leech of the main and / or the jib being too tight. Also, the sails may be too full and the slot may be too closed.

- Make sure you haven't over-sheeted the jib or the main. If you let out the mainsheet you may need to raise the traveller to windward to centre the boom.
- Have a look at the mast bend fore and aft. It may be too straight. Remove chocks from in front of the mast (or loosen the strut). If that doesn't help, rake the spreaders aft a little. The top telltale on the leech of the main should just break.
- Tighten the cunningham(s) to bring the flow forward.
- Tighten the outhaul.
- Check the mast rake. It's probably too upright.
- Also sight up the mast to make sure the mast is not bending to leeward in the middle. If it is, the slot will close. Increase rig tension. If this

doesn't help, shorten the spreaders.
- Check the centreboard. It may be down too far.

2. You can't point, but are fast

The leeches are probably too slack. The top leech telltale on the main should be streaming correctly, i.e. in flat water it should be stalling 60% of the time, in chop it should be stalling 40% of the time.

- Is the mast over-bent? If there are creases (from the clew to the middle of the mast), this is probably the case. Add more chocks in front of the mast (or tighten the strut). Rake the spreaders further forward.
- Check for sideways bend. If the mast is bending to weather in the middle, shorten the spreaders or increase rig tension.
- If the luff of the jib is too full it will stop you pointing. Increase rig tension to prevent luff sag. If necessary, you may have to get the sailmaker to re-cut the jib luff.
- Ease the outhaul.
- Put the centreboard down more. Make sure the centreboard is stiff enough. Check that it is tight in the case.
- Move the jib fairleads inboard.

3. You are low *and* slow

Resist the temptation to give up! Something major is wrong. Do the obvious things first – heel the boat and check for weed, make sure the slot gasket is in place and the centreboard is ok. Then look aloft – has something broken or fallen off?

Is this a new problem? If you were fast before, what could have changed? Is everything on the right setting for today's conditions?

Are you slow on both tacks? If not, then your set up is wrong. When ashore, go through the set up systematically, as described in *The Initial Set-*

Up and *Refining The Set-Up*. Hopefully you will find that something is out of kilter, and can correct it.

If you have no luck you may have to approach an expert in the class to have a look at your boat, and perhaps sail it to understand the issues.

4. You are slow on the reach

- You need full sails so straighten the mast.
- Let off the vang a bit, and ease the cunningham and outhaul (so the lens foot operates).
- Ease the sheets. It's always better to sheet out too much than to be over-sheeted. Trim the jib to the middle pair of telltales.
- Check your body position(s). In light airs you may need to move further forwards.
- Try raising the centreboard more.
- Sail the boat flat, to reduce weather helm.
- Make sure the spinnaker pole is in line with the boom, and the clews of the sail are level.
- Consider the weight of the boat and of the crew. If you are giving a rival 20 kg, they are bound to be faster.

- On a close reach in a breeze tighten the cunningham and the outhaul. Let off the vang. Ease the jibsheet.
- Did you plan ahead and set your smaller, flatter spinnaker?

5. You are slow on the run

- Check your position in the boat. You may need to be further forward.
- Sail the boat flat. In light airs you may need to heel to windward or to leeward to reduce wetted area.
- Ease the sheets.
- Let off the vang and cunningham.
- Pull on the outhaul to give maximum area.
- Push the centreboard up more.
- Reduce the mast rake by easing the shrouds so it is upright or even further forward (see photo, below).
- Ease the spinnaker and square it round as much as possible. Check that your spinnaker is as large as the rules allow.

On the run the mast should be upright or even raked forward, as in the Star

6. You have trouble starting

The key is to set up the boat for the first beat, preferably on a tuning beat with your buddy. Try not to alter these settings in the pre-start period, though you may have to ease the vang if you need to stop the boat. Be sure to have pulled it on again before you sheet in to blast off the line – it's the vang that makes the boat accelerate.

If you are worried about pointing, set up with slightly tighter leeches, a slacker outhaul and a bit more power in the sails. Sheet the jib a bit tighter and tighten the vang a tad. Once you have space to leeward, revert to the settings from your tuning beat.

7. You set up the rig for light airs but the wind has increased

You need to rake the mast back and bend it. If you have an adjustable rig, rake the mast by letting off the jib halyard / forestay and tightening the shrouds. If your controls are limited simply let off the jib halyard / forestay a small amount. Then:

- Remove chocks from in front of the mast (or let off the strut).
- Raise the centreboard (or daggerboard).
- Pull on the vang and cunningham to flatten and twist the main.
- Move the jib fairleads aft.

If you're set up for light winds and it gets up, rake the mast back

8. You set up the rig for heavy airs but the wind has dropped

You need to make the mast more upright and straighten it. Let off the shrouds a little and tighten the jib halyard / forestay, to rake the mast forward. If your controls are limited simply tighten the jib halyard / forestay a bit.

- Insert chocks in front of the mast (or tighten the strut).
- Let off the vang a bit and let off the cunningham completely.
- Ease the outhaul.
- Push down the centreboard.
- Move the jib fairlead forward.

9. You are slow in chop

You need more power, so set the sails fuller and with more twist. Increase crew weight!

- Straighten the mast.
- Drop the boom a little to leeward to give drive through the chop.
- Raise the centreboard a little.
- Move your weight aft a little.
- Don't pinch, foot more.
- Make quick rudder movements / focus on steering the boat over the waves.
- Keep moving the mainsheet in and out all the time.

10. You are slow in waves

Set up for the lighter wind in the troughs. In other words, power up. Steer subtly. Luff going uphill, bear away downhill. Move your body weight back going uphill, forward downhill.

11. You are slow in gusty winds

Your objectives are to keep the boat flat and to stop the sails backwinding:

- Set up with slightly less vang than usual.
- Raise the centreboard a little.

Watch for a gust arriving. As it hits, feather the boat to windward a little, letting out the main and jib sheets. These precautions will keep the boat flat, prevent the wind getting under the hull and keep the boat moving.

Sail Shape

Problem	Cause	Cure
Leech hooked and all talltales stalling	Having the mainsheet too tight	Ease mainsheet tension so at least the top telltale starts to stream
Flow too far forward	Mast too straight	Increase mast bend, angle spreaders further aft
Upper leech falls off	Sail too flat in the head	More kicker tension

Batten Issues

Problem	Cause	Cure
Puckering either side of top batten, and the sail too flat	Having the top batten too loose	Tighten top batten
Top batten hooking to windward	Too much fullness in the head or too much kicker	Reduce fullness or loosen kicking strap
Bubbling either side of top batten pocket, with more fullness in head	Having the top batten too tight	Loosen top batten
Inboard end of lower batten poking up to windward	Possibly too much lower mast bend and outhaul too tight. Bottom of sail too flat	Try releasing the outhaul or look at the cut of the sail

Spreader Issues

Problem	Cause	Cure
Mainsail too flat	Spreaders swept too far aft	Move spreaders further forward
Mast too straight and flow too far forward	Spreaders swept too far forward	Angle spreaders back
Overpowered and less responsive in gusts	Spreaders too long	Reduce length of spreaders
Underpowered with mast bending sideways	Spreaders too short	Lengthen spreaders

Dealing With Creases

Creases sometimes appear in the sails and here I will explain what they mean and what to do about them.

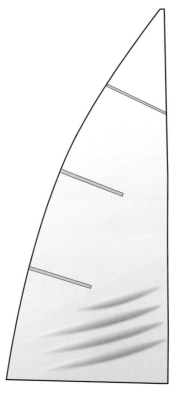 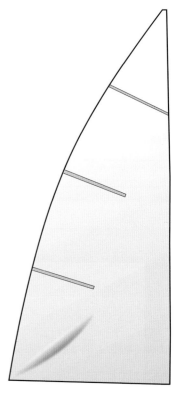

Crease	Crease from the luff	Crease from clew to inboard end of bottom batten / distortion from clew
Cause	Too much lower mast bend	Sail probably old and material past its best. More noticeable in flat sails
Cure	Pull strut down, chock more or increase lowers tension	Buy a new sail!

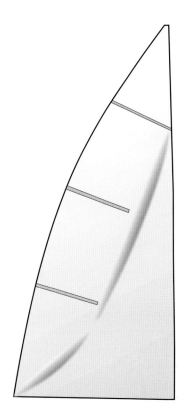 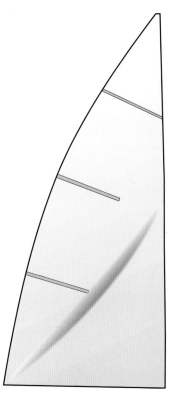 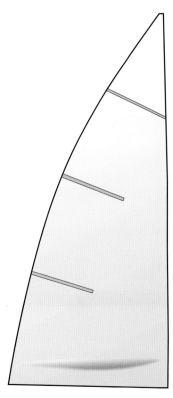

Crease from clew to inboard end of bottom batten and then to inner end of top batten	Crease from clew to mid-mast	Crease along the foot
Not enough luff round in the upper part of the mainsail and a stiff, non-tapered batten can exagerate this	Too much mast bend in the middle of the mast	Tack of mainsail too far back
More luff round and a tapered batten with a slightly softer inboard end	Spreaders further forward	Tighten strop around mast or increase inhaul tension

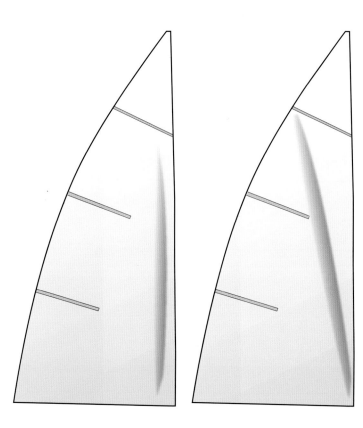

Crease	Crease along the luff	From tack up diagonally
Cause	Main halyard too tight or cunningham on too much	Tack of mainsail pinned, causing crease to outer end of top batten
Cure	Ease or release main halyard or cunningham	Remove tack pin and tie around mast

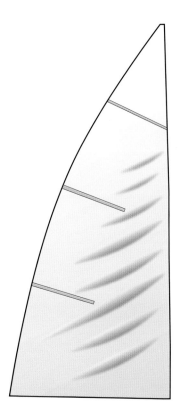  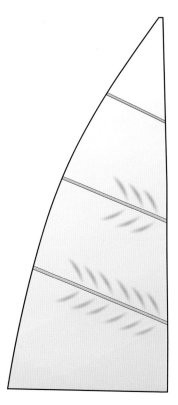

Lots of creases from the middle of the mast	Baggy bits on luff between battens (on fully battened sail)	Creases along the lower battens (on fully battened sail)
Having the kicking strap too tight	Too much luff round for the given stiffness of battens	Not enough batten tension making the sail flatter than necessary
Reduce kicker tension	Increase mast bend or re-cut sail	Increase batten tension

SKILLS

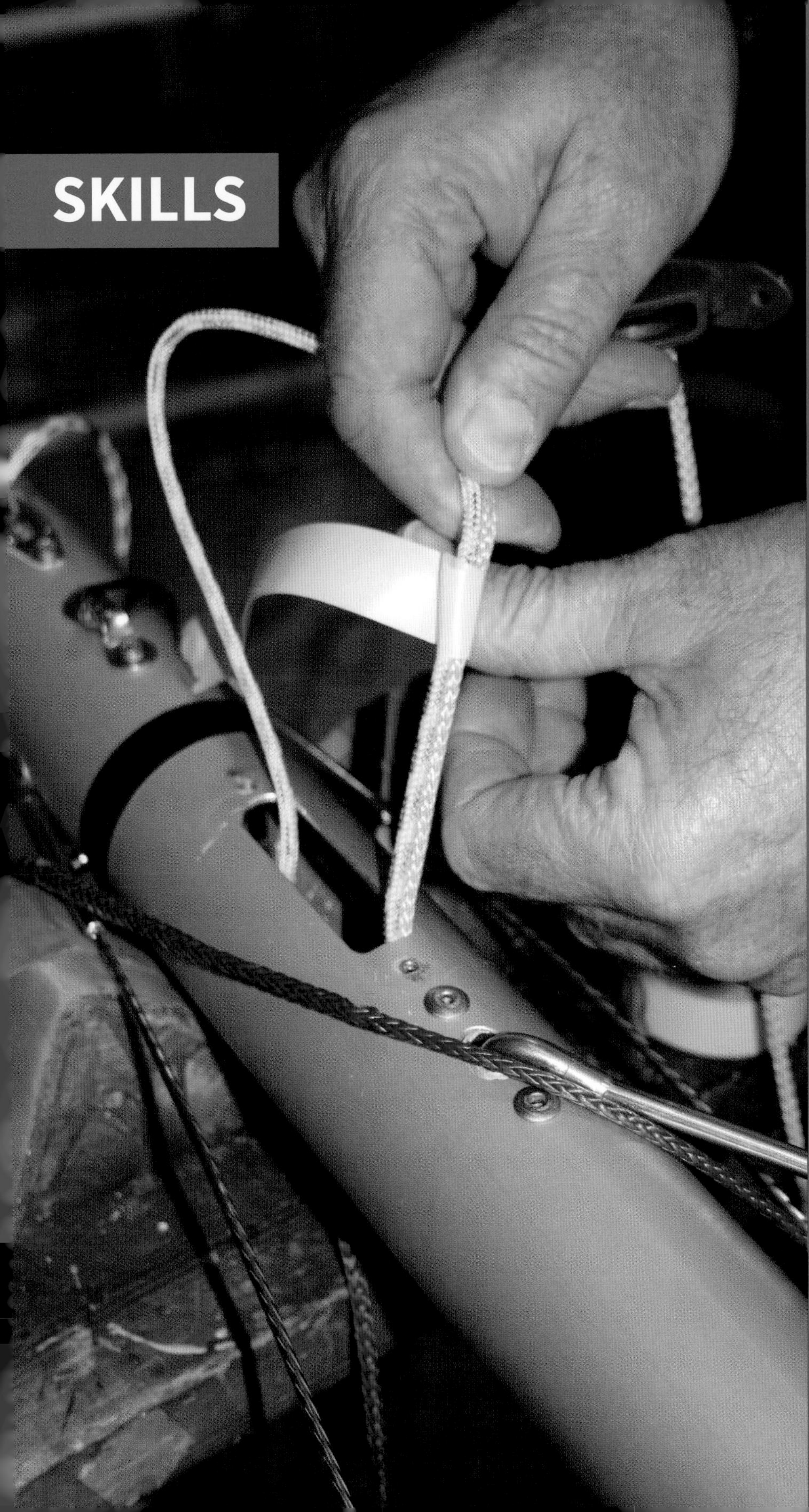

PART 3

Equipment Needed

If you bought a new boat it will, hopefully, be properly set up. But if you need to modify a second-hand boat you will need some skills. And anyway, if something breaks at a regatta, you are going to have to fix it!

We fit out hundreds of boats a year and so have learnt a lot and developed techniques of how to do things. The aim of this section of the book is to give you an insight into these techniques so you can gain from our experience.

Tools

It goes without saying that you should use the very best tools, the sharpest drills and so on – compromising on your tools will compromise the job.

You should always have a basic set of tools with you at a sailing event, and take some of them on the water with you. I would recommend always taking on the water:

- A Gerber multi-tool or shackle key with screwdriver
- A knife

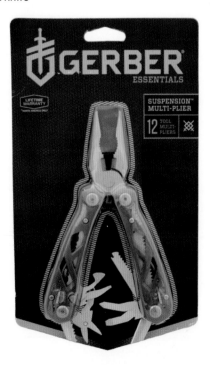

Spares

What and how many spares you carry will depend on your class and where you are sailing.

If you are travelling a long distance for a championship, check whether there will be spares available. Otherwise, if you break something specific to your class (e.g. a lower pintle) your regatta may be over before it's begun.

If there are no spares at the venue, take a spare of anything that can break:

- Pintles
- Boom
- Mast
- Ropes
- Blocks
- Gooseneck
- Tiller
- Rudder blade
- Centreboard
- Shackles
- Cleats
- Your old sails in case something rips

On the water I would take:

- Pins and split rings
- Electric tape
- Spare shackles
- Spare Spectra line

A multi-tool is an essential piece of on-the-water equipment

Attaching Fittings To The Hull

When attaching fittings to the hull you should usually use bolts. On a fibreglass hull you also need a wooden pad behind the fibreglass. You can screw into this, but usually you would bolt fittings using penny washers and locking nuts. For a wooden boat it is still best to bolt fittings, but you can use wood screws otherwise. In either case, if the load is high you must use bolts. Don't overtighten them or you may crush the foam, or even the fibreglass. And always use stainless steel fittings!

If you don't know where the wooden pads are phone the builder or, if you have to, drill small holes to check.

If you need to fix a wooden pad in an inaccessible place, drill small holes and thread strings through. Use these to pull a glued pad hard against the inside of the hull or deck. When dry, you can drill through into the new pad.

Use Sikaflex (a flexible sealant, or Silicone rubber) under each fitting – it's waterproof and does a bit of bonding too.

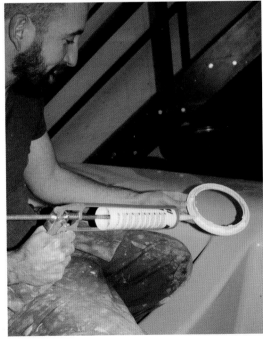

Use a Silicone sealant as it is waterproof and provides some bonding

Sometimes the nut needs to be attached well inside a buoyancy tank. Use your ingenuity: you can tape a spanner to a pole (1), and use mastic (2) to hold the nut in the spanner's jaws (3).

Attaching a nut in a difficult-to-reach place

If you need a long bolt use a piece of studding (a long, threaded rod). Cut it to the correct length, and cut a groove in the top end so you can twist it with a screwdriver.

Fitting Slot Gaskets

There are two types of gasket: a Mylar sheet which you glue on, and sailcloth which is held by battens.

To fit a Mylar gasket:

- Choose a warm, dry environment.
- Choose correct width of Mylar, giving about 15 mm overlap outside the case.
- Draw the slit and an inverted V at the aft end, but don't cut it yet (1).
- Drill a small hole at the forward end of where the slit will be to stop the split spreading.
- De-grease the glueing area and roughen the surface (2&3).
- Coat the hull and Mylar with contact adhesive (3M is recommended) (4).
- Mask the area around the adhesive (5).
- Position the gasket and press down.
- Cut out the inverted V at the aft end to leave a small hole at the end of the centreboard case which sucks water out of the case when sailing.
- Remove the masking. When dry, cut along the centreline using scissors.
- Put Dacron adhesive over the front leading edge to prevent Mylar from lifting or coming away (6).

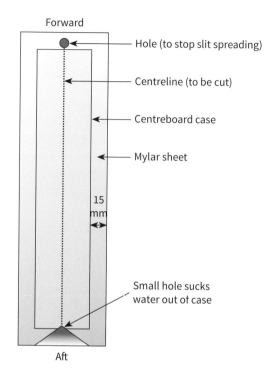

Forward

Hole (to stop slit spreading)

Centreline (to be cut)

Centreboard case

Mylar sheet

15 mm

Small hole sucks water out of case

Aft

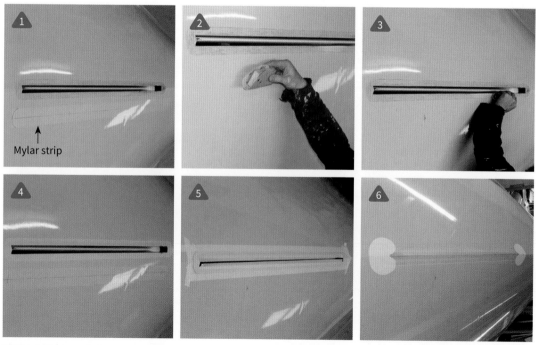

Fitting a Mylar gasket

To fit a sailcloth gasket:

- Measure and mark up the centre of the centreboard hole at the aft end (1) and forward end (2).
- Arrange the sailcloth in a U shape, screwing the ends in place at the front of the case (3).
- Fix a string to the rudder pintles and use it to stretch the middle of the sailcloth along the case (4).
- Gradually screw on each keelband, working from the front towards the back (5) until it is all screwed on (6).
- Cut the string and then mark up (7) and cut (8) the aft end in an inverted V. The small hole this creates sucks water out of the case when the boat is sailing.
- Trim the edges (9).

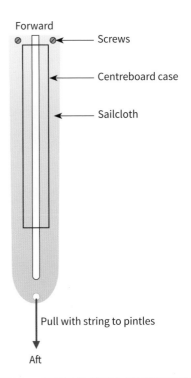

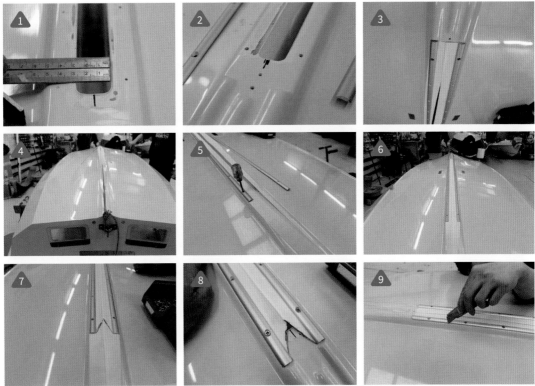

Fitting a sailcloth gasket

To fit a rubber gasket:

If the rules allow, you should also consider fitting a rubber gasket at the front end of the centreboard. We use a single piece of latex, cut in a V shape. This gives good flow around the leading edge of the centreboard, and closes the gap when the board is angled aft.

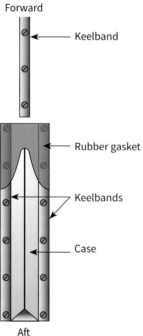

The latex rubber gasket gives good flow round the leading edge of the centreboard

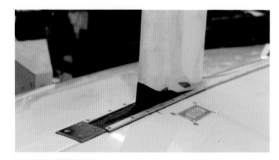

Siting & Attaching A Cleat

Make sure each rope goes squarely through its cleat, not at an angle. Use an angled packer (i.e. a wedge) to pad the cleat until it lines up. Use a parallel packer if you need to raise the cleat so that you can pull the rope into its jaws without hitting anything (e.g. the deck). Also make sure that the lead is such that it helps the rope stay in the jaws – if you get the alignment wrong the tension in the rope can pull it out of the cleat.

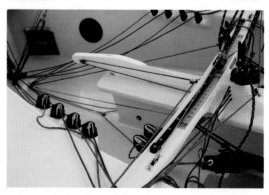

Using angled and parallel packers to site a cleat

Fitting Transom Flaps

- Cut polycarbonate 'flaps' 10-12 mm bigger than the holes in the transom, and with more overlap at the top edge.
- Drill two small holes in the centre of each flap and thread the elastic.
- Stick a pro-grip 'hinge' to attach a spacer to the top of each flap and drill 2 holes in the spacer (1).

- Position each spacer above its hole in the transom (2).
- Check alignment with the hole in the transom (3).
- Bolt (or screw) each spacer to the transom (4).
- Attach the elastic from each flap over a hook on the cockpit floor / hog – the tension in the elastic holds the flaps shut (5).
- When the elastic is released after a capsize, the flaps will open and let the water out (6).

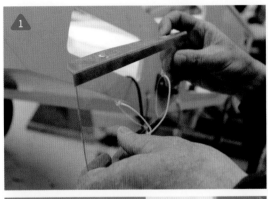
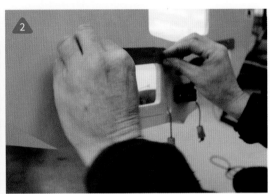

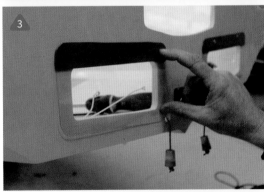

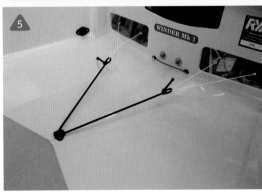
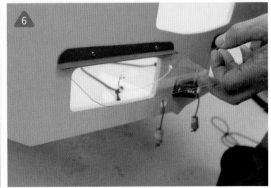

Fitting transom flaps

Ropework

If you follow the advice in this book you will be using the control lines all the time, so they must work efficiently. The biggest obstacle to this is using rope that is too thick. Wear gloves, then use the thinnest rope possible. And make sure each rope goes squarely through its cleat (see p92).

Modern cored ropes, like Dyneema, are much more difficult to splice than the old three-stranded variety, so this is a skill you need to learn.

Using A Fid

Fids are used in splicing. The photo below shows fids of different sizes – for use with ropes of different diameters. Note each has a spike in the gutter. You push one rope into the gutter and the spike grips it while the fid is pushed through another rope, or through the initial rope itself.

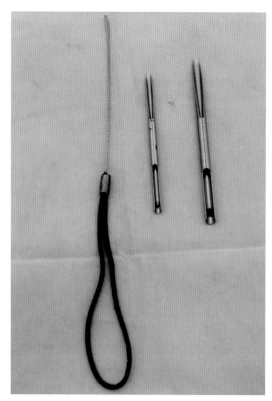

Fids for splicing

Making A Locking Loop In Dyneema

See photo sequence opposite.
- Make a loop and mark it with a felt tip pen (1 & 2).
- Push the fid through the short tail (3).
- Load the fid with the tail and pull it through (4).
- Push the fid through the long tail again and use it to pull the short tail through (5).
- Push the fid through the long tail longitudinally (6).
- Feed the loose tail into the fid, then pull the fid and the rope out, so that the short tail is completely inside the long tail (7).
- Now you have a loop with no end showing (8). If there is a little tail, cut it off.

Note that you can only make a locking splice at one end of the rope because you have to feed the other end of the rope through the rope.

Making A Loop At The Other End Of The Rope

See photo sequence opposite.
- Mark the loop.
- Push the fid through the long tail and load the short tail onto it. Pull the short tail through (1).
- Repeat twice (2), so that you have pulled the short tail through three times (3).
- Finally push the fid through the core of the long tail and use it to pull the short tail into the long one (4).

The loop will slip if there is no tension on it, so stitch through the splice to lock it.

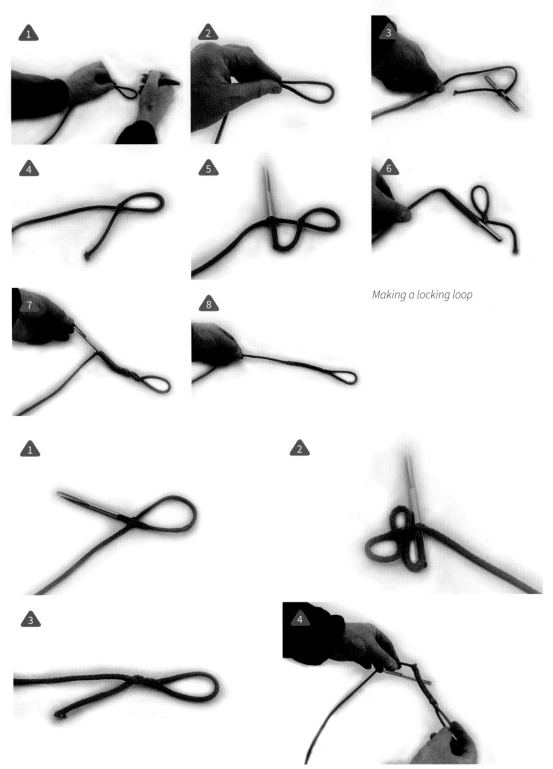

Making a locking loop

Making a loop at the other end of the rope

Making An Adjustable Loop
(e.g. for the mainsheet strop)

- Make the loop and mark the tails with a felt tip pen (1).
- Feed the fid down the long tail from the mark (you may need to 'milk' the rope a bit) (2).
- Feed the short tail into the fid and use the fid to pull the short tail through the long tail (3).
- Pull the short tail through until the marks are aligned (4).
- Tie a thumb knot on the short tail to stop it sliding through (5).

To shorten the loop, simply pull the end and tie another knot. In fact it is a good idea to make marks for light, medium and strong wind settings of the loop – the idea being to keep the boom central despite the rake altering.

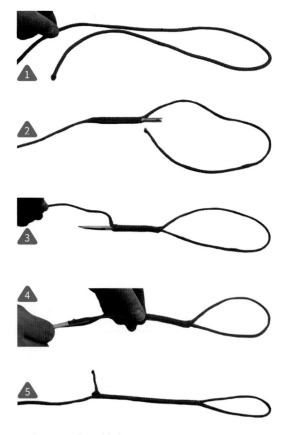

Making an adjustable loop

Splicing Two Ends Of A Rope Together (e.g. to make a continuous control line)

- Cross the ends over each other, leaving equal tails (**A** and **B**) (1).
- Push the fid through the standing part of **B** and use it to pull tail **A** through (2).
- Push the fid through the standing part of **A** and use it to pull tail **B** through (3).
- Repeat this once more for each tail (4). Now the splice is locked (5).

- Now get rid of the ends. Thread the fid through the length of rope **A**, and load it with tail **B**. Withdraw the fid, pulling tail **B** inside rope **A** (6). Get rid of tail **A** in a similar way.
- Concertina the splice and pull out each tail a bit. Trim them off (7), then 'milk' the splice so the ends are completely internal (8).

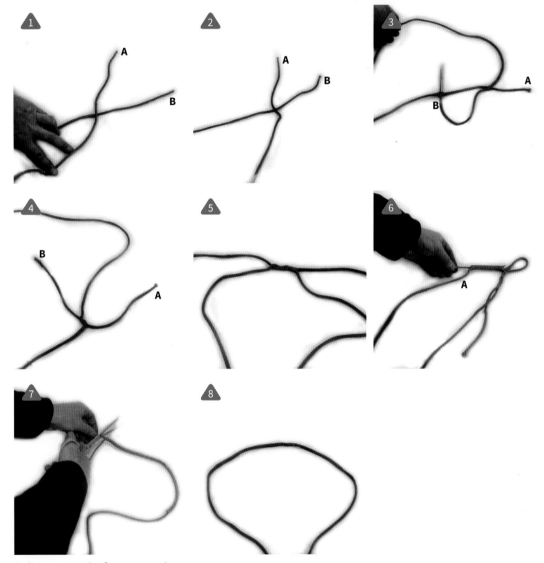

Splicing two ends of a rope together

Making A Vang Cascade System

- Pull up the mainsail and, with no downward pressure on the boom, measure between the vang take-off points on the boom and the mast.
- Hammer two nails into a flat surface this distance apart, to make two pegs around which you can make the cascade (1).
- Make a locking splice around the mast take-off (2).
- Hang a block from the other peg and run the rope through it. Add a bobble, and splice it to a second block so the rope is tight when the blocks are touching. The bobble stops the rope jamming when the vang is let off (3).

Repeat for the next part of the cascade, and so on. Most boats will need 16:1. The final blocks may need to be double if there is insufficient run.

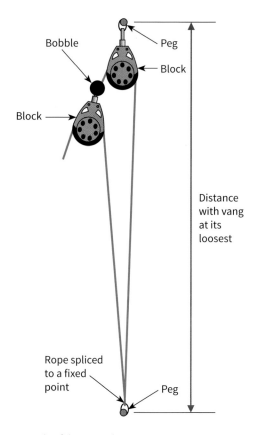

Principle of the cascade system

Making a vang cascade system

Boat & Foil Repairs

You will occasionally damage your boat or the foils, so in this section I will give you a few tips on how to make repairs.

Identifying A Leak

- Put a foot pump in the bung hole and pump in air.
- Listen for air being released or put soapy water on suspected areas and look for bubbles.
- Make sure there are seals on the hatch covers.
- Check the hull-to-deck joints, particularly after a collision.
- Check fittings which may have become loose.

Repairing Dings In A Glass Hull

- Grind out all loose or cracked gelcoat using a power file.
- If the glass underneath is damaged grind that out too.
- Apply glass.
- Fair, then apply gelcoat.
- Fair that, then polish.

To polish, use 3M polish (cutting compound) and a polishing mop (like a slow speed sander).

Repairing Dings In Foils

Repairing A Damaged Leading Edge
- Grind out a bigger area around the ding (1).
- Prepare resin (2) and fill the gap with resin (3).
- Grind off the surface of the repair (4).
- Use fine sandpaper to create a smooth finish (5 & 6).

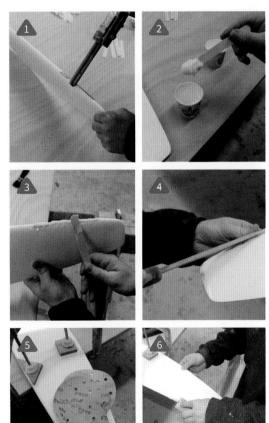

Some damage will require a professional repair

Reapairing a damaged leading edge

Repairing A Damaged Trailing Edge

If the ding is on the trailing edge any quick repair tends to fall off, because there is not much bonding area. You need to:

- Grind out a bigger area around the ding.
- Stick glass tape over both sides and fill the gap with resin (see diagram below).
- Grind off the whole surface of the repair.
- Apply gel coat or paint.
- Use fine sandpaper to create a smooth finish.

The photo sequence for repairing a broken bottom corner (right) illustrates the steps.

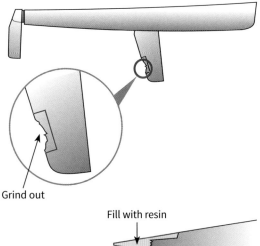

Grind out

Fill with resin

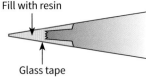

Glass tape

Repairing A Broken Corner

- Grind out a bigger area around the ding (1 & 2).
- Stick glass tape over both sides (3) and apply resin (4).
- Clamp until dry (5).
- Trim edges (6).
- Grind off the surface of the repair (7).
- Apply gel coat or paint (8 & 9).
- Use fine sandpaper to create a smooth finish (10).

Reapairing a broken corner

Taking The Centreboard In & Out

This is something that many people struggle with.
- Before you take out the board put a mark at the same place on the board and on the top of the centreboard case where they meet so that you know how the board should line up.
- Before you put the board back, mark a cross through the hole in the board.
- When you put the board back in, line up the marks on the board and thwart.
- Look through the case when you put the board back in and use the cross to help find the hole.
- Finally push the bolt through.

Put a cross through the hole on the board

Reducing Slack In The Rudder & Centreboard

Use chafe tape to pack the rudder head until it fits the stock. The tape comes in two thicknesses: 250 microns and 500 microns. It is very sticky on one side and very slippery on the other.

You can also use this tape for packing the centreboard, and for padding the deck where lines are chewing it up.

Chafe tape helps pack the centreboard but also aids movement

Rigging

In general, the rigging stays up and won't cause you any problems, but when a halyard breaks or a shroud goes you need to take action. I hope this section will give you a few tips for these occasions.

How To Order New Shrouds

The loft will set up two pegs on their work surface to show the length of the shroud from bearing point to bearing point. This is the dimension you want to give them, NOT the overall length of the shroud.

Note that they should use an eye thimble in each end, because this won't deform (stretch). If they use a split thimble it will elongate and your shrouds will lengthen under pressure.

Swage eye (the solid one): for high performance boats

Solid thimble: an alternative for less high performance boats

Split thimble: avoid because it may distort

Getting A New Main Halyard Through The Mast

If the old halyard is still in place, use it to pull the new one through by taping the two together. If not, you may be able to use the spinnaker halyard to pull the new main halyard through:

- Remove the pulley where the spinnaker halyard exits near the top of the mast.
- Push a length of wire into the mast here. Keep pushing until it exits at the top.
- Use the wire to pull the new main halyard round the top sheave and out of the spinnaker halyard's hole.
- Fasten the halyards together here.
- Pull the spinnaker halyard out of the bottom of the mast so it drags the main halyard down the mast.
- Hook the main halyard out of its sheave near the bottom of the mast and detach the spinnaker halyard.

If you are replacing the jib halyard you follow a similar process, as is shown in the photo sequence (right):

- Remove the pulley where the jib halyard exits the mast (1-5).
- Use a metal loop to pull out the spinnaker halyard (6-9).
- Fasten the new jib halyard to the spinnaker halyard (10-11).
- Pull the spinnaker halyard out of the bottom of the mast so it drags the jib halyard with it (12).

A ←   → **B**

Measure the shroud from bearing point A to bearing point B

- Hook the jib halyard out of its sheave near the bottom of the mast and detach the spinnaker halyard.

In a new mast, push a wire right through. Attach all the halyards to it and pull them through the mast together – they are less likely to twist like this. (You can also use this technique if you have twisted halyards, i.e. pull them all out and start again!)

Note that I don't recommend dropping a plumb line down the mast, perhaps using the sailing club balcony to get high enough. You see many people doing this, but they are likely to twist the halyards inside the mast.

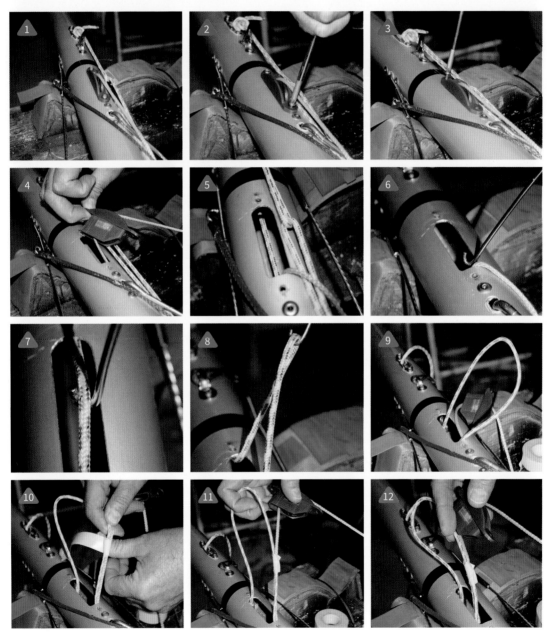

Threading a jib halyard

Sail Care & Repairs

Sails are the engine of your boat, so it is important that you look after them (which will avoid premature damage) and know how to repair them when it becomes necessary.

Sail Care

Upon Completion Of A Race

Once ashore, sea sailors should wash their sails in fresh water to remove the salt, and both inland and sea sailors should dry them as soon as possible. The best way to dry sails is to lay them on a clean floor / grass or draped over the boat, rather than leaving them up to flog in the wind as this is one of the quickest way to ruin your sails. In wet weather the easiest way to dry them at home is by laying them out on the floor.

Rolling Mainsail & Foresails

Once you have dried your sails, or if temporarily putting them away when wet, you should roll them. This is the best way of storing your sails. To roll your sail you should shake all the creases out. DO NOT pull them out otherwise you will put permanent creases into the sail. Once laid flat, roll the mainsail from the headboard down the leech in line with the battens (leave your battens in). The foresail should be treated the same way but rolled down the luff, taking care not to kink the luff wire.

All the patches and batten pockets are on one side of the sail, so when you roll the sail have them

Roll a sail with the patches and batten pockets on the inside

on the inside of your roll, otherwise the rolled sail will be far more bulky.

On a boat like a 29er, the jib leech line shrinks: it is important to let it off when rolling the sails and then re-tie it on for sailing.

Let off the jib leech line before folding the sail

Take care not to fold or crease the window in either the main or foresail, especially in cold weather. It is important to take care of modern-day cloth as it has a very hard finish, meaning that the sail needs extra care not to fold creases into the sail otherwise little white score marks will appear. These score marks cannot always be avoided: they are inevitable as the sail is used, however they do not affect the performance or strength of the sail, just the cosmetic character.

Spinnakers

The best way to fold a spinnaker is by placing the leeches together then folding the centrefold in line with the leech. Halve the sail once more in the same way then roll from the head.

If the sails are rolled or folded correctly they will emerge the next time smooth and free of all but the minimum of marks.

Cleaning

DO NOT use hot water to wash the sails, just warm. Never use strong detergents, just household soap to sponge away marks. The best way to remove oil is to use triclothylene or swarfega. Sails can be kept in tip-top condition by removing stains and dirt as they collect.

Sail Repair

For any sizeable sail repair you are always going to be best going back to your sailmaker, but sometimes there isn't the time, opportunity or money available.

Repairing A Hole In The Spinnaker

- Lay out the clean, dry spinnaker so it's flat.
- Cut a spare bit of material into a patch, with rounded corners.
- Spread silicone rubber onto the patch and stick it onto the spinnaker. (A patch on one side is enough.)
- Let it dry.

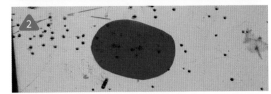

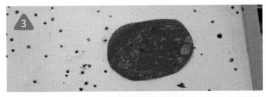

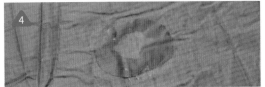

Repairing A Hole In The Mainsail Or Jib

If the area is non-stressed, use a Dacron adhesive strip. Simply peel off the back and stick it on.

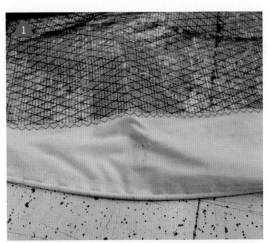

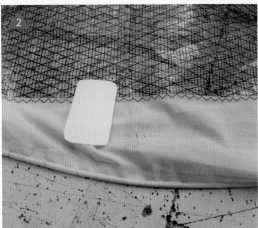

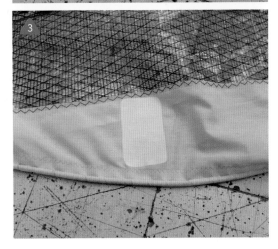

When repairing a hole caused by the spreader:
- Cut out a circle to cover the hole (1).
- Stick the patch over the hole (2).

For a rip caused by stress, e.g. where the cunningham has been pulled too hard, use Mylar repair tape:
- Cut out the appropriate length of Mylar repair tape (1).
- Apply the tape, where possible lining up the warp lines to give more strength (2).

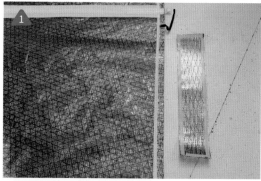

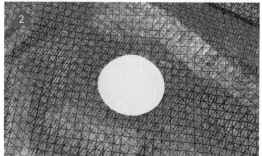

If the reinforcing comes adrift (1), apply Dacron adhesive to stick it back down (2).

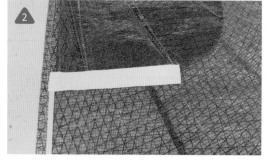

END NOTE

In this book we have covered the three key areas involved in increasing your boatspeed:

Part 1: Assembling the gear and understanding what each control does.

Part 2: How to set up your boat for light wind beating, and then how to adjust this for different wind strengths and points of sail.

Part 3: The skills you need to work on your boat to make sure it is optimally fitted out.

Like anything in life, the more time you spend tuning, the faster you will go. How much effort you put in will depend on your aspirations:

- If you want to win an Olympic medal you will need the time to prepare the boat on a daily basis, and log every setting. Then if something breaks you can get a spare up and running fast, even between races.
- If you want to win a championship, you will want to work on the boat weekly, rather than daily, but you will need to really understand how to tune your boat to the optimum.
- Many of you will simply be looking to improve your performance and perhaps win the occasional race. For you, any better understanding and implementation of tuning will reap dividends.

Remember, just 2% more boatspeed is likely to see you leaping up the fleet!

Ian Pinnell
2016

SAIL TO WIN

"Don't *just* sail... **SAIL TO WIN!**"

Other titles in this series

Wind Strategy
David Houghton &
Fiona Campbell

The go-to wind book
since 1986, this new-look
edition is fully updated for
modern forecasting and
analyses popular racing
venues around the world.

Helming to Win
Nick Craig

A breakthrough book
from the 'Champion of
Champions', Nick Craig,
which will catapult
you from club racer to
championship winner.

Coach Yourself to Win
Jon Emmett

The twelve fundamental
elements of successful
sailing from a gold medal
winning coach and sailor,
with additional advice
from Olympic medallists.

Sign up to our mailing list at **www.fernhurstbooks.com** to register
your interest in racing. We will keep you up-to-date with our latest
news, details of new books & exclusive special offers.

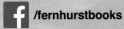 **/fernhurstbooks**   **@FernhurstBooks**   **Fernhurst Books**